William J. Fay

First
Corinthians

Spiritual Commentaries on the Bible

New Testament Editor

Mary Ann Getty-Sullivan

Vincent P. Branick

First Corinthians

Building Up the Church

New City Press

Published in the United States by New City Press
202 Cardinal Rd., Hyde Park, NY 12538
©2001 Vincent P. Branick

Cover design by Nick Cianfarani
The cover picture, "All of Creation" (16th c.), is used with permission
of Orthodox Byzantine Icons.

Nihil Obstat: Rev. Paul P. Zilonka, C.P., S.T.D.
Imprimatur: Rev. Msgr. W. Francis Malooly, V.G., Archdiocese of Baltimore

Library of Congress Cataloging-in-Publication Data:
  Branick, Vincent P.
    First Corinthians : building up the church / Vincent Branick.
      p. cm.
    ISBN 1-56548-162-3
      1. Bible. N.T. Corinthians, 1st--Commentaries. I. Title

  BS2675.3 .B73 2001
  227'.2077--dc21   2001037000

Printed in Canada

To my three sons

Christopher, Kevin, and Sean

Contents

Introduction

Paul has been in Ephesus for about two years when at least two delegations arrived from the Christians at Corinth just across the Aegean Sea. It is about the year A.D. 55 just before Pentecost, the spring feast fifty days after Passover (16:8). Complaints about factions and disunity are coming from Cloe, a wealthy woman, head of a household who had sent a group of her servants and slaves over to Paul (1:11). Another prominent household head, Stephanas, along with two of his servants, Fortunatus and Achaicus, also arrive with a series of questions and other concerns (16:17).

Paul would have preferred to speak to the Corinthian community in person. In fact, he has now determined to go to Corinth and spend some time there (16:5–6). But for the moment he does the next best thing. He writes a letter—as he had done earlier (5:9). This letter, however, would have to cover a number of topics, from serious moral problems at Corinth to issues of squeamish consciences.

The Church of Corinth

Like Ephesus Corinth was a big city, a port city. Its population, estimated as high as 600,000, included the very rich who lived in opulent villas and lavished their wealth on beneficence, like Erastus, the Aedile, who paved the large plaza near the theater at his own expense. The city also included the very poor who either lived with their families in hovels or gathered with other families in dank tenement apartments. This was a city where slaves were in the two-thirds majority.

Jewish Christians were in Corinth already in A.D. 52 when Paul arrived with Timothy and Silvanus (also known as Silas).

Luke describes Paul's arrival in Corinth in Acts 18:1–21. Prisca (a.k.a. Priscilla) and Aquila were among those Jewish Christians expelled from Rome by Claudius some three years earlier when disputes about Christ within the Jewish community alarmed the political authorities. Thus this couple were happy to offer Paul and his companions hospitality in their Corinthian villa. It was just such a household that Paul needed as a base of operations.

The community that quickly grew around the dynamic work of Paul reflected the stress and strains of the city's population. These stresses reflected the divisions between the wealthy and the poor, between the highly disciplined and the immoral, between those who sought the honor and prestige so important in Roman society and those who had no hope of such honor.

Even when gathered together, the community was not a large group. Gaius could host the whole community in his dining room for the Lord's Supper (Rom 16:23). When he removed all the couches and large vases so the group could spill out of the dining room into the central courtyard, as many as fifty could gather. But Paul was not a nose counter. What mattered in this *church* was the quality of love and service that united them into a body.

That quality apparently was lacking. Instead this group seemed delighted with the spiritual power that appeared to make it special. Here was a community of prophets and speakers in tongues like no other Paul knew. He did not want to quench this spirit. But he needed to direct their efforts toward the essential of Christian social life, a life of love and service.

Paul's Presuppositions

Although Paul tries to explain his view of Christian life, many of the elements of that view were either so well accepted by his hearers or so pervasive in his thinking that he does not stop to explain them. Yet, our understanding of these elements is crucial for our grasp of Paul's theology—especially if these elements are not pervasive in our thinking.

Apocalyptic dualism. Like many of the devout Jews of his time, like possibly Jesus himself in his human consciousness, Paul saw the universe as the battleground under the ultimate power of God between two cosmic forces, light and darkness, good and evil, the kingdom of God and the kingdom of Satan. Paul rarely refers to Satan. He prefers to name these forces by more abstract images. In First Thessalonians he used the categories of "light" and "darkness" (5:4–5). In First Corinthians Paul tries out another antithesis, *pneumatikos* ("spiritual") and *psychikos* ("natural"?). Paul uses this antithesis to describe the difference between the corruptible body we now have which must die (*psychikos*) and the incorruptible body risen from the dead which shares eternal glory (*pneumatikos*) (15:42–44). This is also the antithesis Paul uses to distinguish the person (*psychikos*) for whom the gifts of God seem foolish from the person (*pneumatikos*) who understands the gifts of God, and especially who sees the crucifixion of Jesus as God's power and wisdom (1:18–2:16). The difference between these two types of people is the presence of God's Spirit, the power of the new age. Paul sees the difference not simply as a matter of ethical conduct, but as a matter of being. Ethical conduct is the Christian response to this transformation of the spirit.

Apocalyptic urgency. For Paul "time is running out" (7:29). This apocalyptic urgency percolates into Paul's theology from his Jewish background. Just as Jesus had proclaimed, "The Kingdom of God is at hand!" so likewise pious Jews of Paul's world saw their generation as the last. Paul, however, had a particular reason for thinking that the great eschatological climax should come soon. He had experienced the risen Christ, and in Christ's resurrection he saw the beginning of the End. Christ's resurrection was the beginning of a series, "the first fruits of those who have fallen asleep" (15:20). In the small piece of reality called Jesus of Nazareth, God had begun the process of transforming his creation from the corruption of sin and death. It would seem that the rest of transformation of creation would have to happen soon.

The church as the beachhead of the Kingdom. Through the Spirit and through sharing the bread and cup of the Lord's Supper—in later letters Paul will list other means—Christians plug into Christ and his eschatological transformation. This is God's grace "bestowed in Christ Jesus" (1:4). As a community Christians can thus begin living the social life of God's Kingdom, a life of love, a life of mutual edification, a life of the Spirit. Table fellowship with Jesus should be a time when Christians experience a profound union with each other (10:16–17). The community sharing of the gifts should be a time when outsiders witness a glimpse of the Kingdom (14:23–25).

God as redeeming. For Paul the author of redemption is God, the Father. God redeems and saves humanity through Jesus who becomes the medium, not the author, of redemption and salvation. Paul's vision is theocentric. It is God the Father who remains in the center of his faith vision. In later letters Paul will say this more explicitly. In many different ways, however, this central role of God the Father lays as an essential presupposition of First Corinthians. The ultimate triumph of God, as portrayed in this letter, entails ultimately Jesus being subordinate to God, that "God might be all in all" (15:28).

Paul's Theological Vocabulary

The theological vocabulary particularly important for understanding First Corinthians overlaps some of the key words we have seen in the other letters. However, as he was developing his response to the readers of these letters, the following terms were crucial:

Body. The human body is the person in his or her concrete reality. In this letter Paul does not seem to know of any "soul" part of a human being distinct from body. "Body" must not be confused with "flesh" in Paul's vocabulary. Flesh is the dimension of corruptibility and weakness which affects our bodies.

14

For Paul, while there is a resurrection of the body, there is no resurrection, no redemption of the "flesh." But the body is susceptible to God's redemption. It can pass from a fleshy body to a spiritual body by the resurrection. Paul also speaks of a social body, as in our expression, "student body," a meaning as common in Paul's day as in ours.

Church. The word primarily means "assembly," that is, something that goes out of existence when the assembly disperses. Secondarily, for Paul the word means the people that assemble, a reality with a bit more permanence. In this letter it refers to city-wide assemblies. Once it seems to refer to a worldwide group that never really assembles but knows itself as a unified people (10:32). It never means the building in which the group assembles.

Spirit. For Paul this word almost always refers to God's Spirit. Even where Paul clearly refers to a human spirit (5:3–5), he is naming that part of a human being which is open to God. Normally Paul is referring to an intimate aspect of God, named for its life-giving character and its surprising character. The Spirit is above all the power of ultimate (eschatological) salvation.

Spiritual Gifts. Paul uses this term to describe the functions and offices within the church, ranging from various authority positions like that of apostles and prophets to miraculous healing powers and not so miraculous service. By calling them "spiritual" (*pneumatikoi*), Paul indicates their eschatological character. By calling them "gifts" (*charismata*), Paul insists on their origin in God's freedom.

Paul's Way of Expository Writing

Paul attempts to develop ideas and positions in his writing. At first reading, however, this development seems haphazard and disorganized—at least to our minds. The problem lies primarily in the fact that Paul does not write in paragraphs. He does not simply present an idea or position and then with a series of subsequent sentences analyze the idea or relate it to other matters, before going on to the next idea.

Rather Paul often says something then often repeats the same idea in different words or from another angle. For example, Paul writes, "I urge you brothers . . . that all of you agree in what you say, that there be no divisions among you, but that you be united in the same mind and in the same purpose" (1:10). The first and the third repetition are both positive statements. This is known as "synonymous parallelism." The second repetition, however, is a restatement of the same idea by denying the opposite. This is known as "antithetical parallelism." By recognizing the parallel statements we can use one to understand the other.

Sometimes Paul interrupts the parallel by going on to something else, then later returning to the first idea. This type of composition, very common in the ancient world, was a way of relating ideas together by weaving the thoughts around each other. The ancient masters suggested two ways of weaving ideas. One was a kind of bookends composition, the other, a kind of parallel alternation.

The bookends composition or "inclusion," results in a type of A-B-A' pattern. It not only provides an interesting parallelism, but indicates a unit of related thoughts. Note how Paul starts and closes the opening prayer by the name "Christ Jesus . . . Jesus Christ" (1:4–9). A major section of the letter begins with Paul's concern about meat offered to idols (8:1–13) and ends by the same topic (10:23–33). A composition teacher today would demand Paul tighten up the unity of his composition. Just the same, the teacher would have given him a high mark for indicating the subunits of his letter.

Sometimes, a series of bookends inside each other link up several thoughts in a form of inverse symmetry. This type of construction results in a pattern like A-B-C-B'-A'. Today, scholars call that elaborate inversion a "chiasm" after the form of the Greek letter chi, which looks like a big X. Note, for instance, the development, "I have not used any of these rights

. . . an obligation has been imposed on me . . . woe is me if I do not preach it . . . I have been entrusted with a stewardship. . . . I offer the gospel free of charge so as not to make full use of my right in the gospel" (9:15–18).

The second major form of weaving ideas together simply alternates between ideas. Like the great writers of his day, Paul often develops a thought by returning to the same ideas in the same order: A-B-A'-B'. Scholars call also this form of development "parallelism." The parallel alternation can be short and simple: "We are fools on Christ's account, but you are wise in Christ; we are weak, but you are strong" (4:10). Or the parallelism can be subtle and extended. Thus Paul writes,

A. "Our ancestors were all under the cloud and all passed through the sea,

B. and all of them were baptized into Moses in the cloud and in the sea.

A.' All ate the same spiritual food, and all drank the same spiritual drink

B.' for they drank from a spiritual rock that followed them, and the rock was the Christ" (10:1–4).

A-A' describes stories in the Law, the passage through the Red Sea and God's care in the desert. B-B' gives a Pauline interpretation going beyond the story and that relating the biblical narration to Christian realities. He is saying the same thing twice but with different nuances. The key to understanding this rhetoric is to identify the corresponding parts of Paul's exposition and then make comparisons between them. If the idea is important, Paul will say it several times.

The Literary Form of First Corinthians

First Corinthians is a letter. As a letter it is a somewhat spontaneous response to some urgent issues of a very specific group. As a letter it reads somewhat the way a person speaks—freely, often very creatively, in a probing manner, always concerned with the response of the ones addressed. First Corinthians is *not* an essay, written to express and preserve in writing some ideas or information as precisely and accurately as one can, written to anyone, anywhere who will read it, even to someone far in the future. This letter character poses a major challenge to us who wish the truth of this writing to speak to us, to us who wish to actualize this letter.

At the same time of course, First Corinthians is an apostolic letter. Paul was convinced of his extraordinary authority—even though he consistently beseeches rather than commands. He was writing to a local church as a whole. While personal, this letter is anything but private. We hear the voice of an apostle addressing a group of the first generation of Christians struggling to understand the extraordinary grace that had just been bestowed on them and on the world.

Another wrinkle to the literary form of First Corinthians needs to be looked at. This long letter seems to have sections that were composed before and after Paul actually wrote it. These are the "lumpy" parts of the letter—the parts that stand out by a sudden shift of style or form, the parts that have borders similar to stitches which sow them into the letter as a whole, the parts that contain elements in some tension with elements in the rest of the letter.

One lumpy part consists of a section that runs roughly from 1:18 to 2:16 (probably also including 3:18–21). This section is quite Pauline, very consistent with Paul's theology and vocabulary. However, it suddenly shifts to the literary form of a rabbinic homily with snatches of scripture woven together by key words in an intense discourse about the wisdom of the Spirit. No mention is made about church unity, the major theme just before and after this section. Paul may have composed this "homily" before writing to the Corinthians.

The same analysis may be said of chapter 13 which also appears as a lump in its context. It is an intense poem to "love." The section is only loosely connected with chapters 12 and 14, and the meaning of "prophecy" at 13:2 shifts in comparison to Paul's use of the term in chapter 14. Other sections which Paul may have written earlier and then inserted include 6:9–11 and 10:1–13.

To recognize these sections as inserted by Paul is important for interpretation. This view means we should see more in these sections than simply their contextual meaning. There is more to see in Paul's homily on the wisdom of the Spirit than simply an exhortation toward unity. It also means that the historian must be careful using the material in this section to reconstruct the situation in Corinth. How many books and articles have been written speculating about *gnosis*, a cultic "knowledge," in Corinth based on the mention of the "mature" and the "wisdom in mystery" in chapter 2?

Paul obviously did not have a "cut and paste" button on his papyrus. But he did have a great memory. And he knew that the answer to the Corinthians' problems was often in a profound truth that could be expressed only by repeating—and adapting—a composition presented perhaps to a very different group for a very different occasion.

An additional lump in First Corinthians is even more important to recognize. At 14:33b–35 the tension is so great between what is said within this section with Paul's statement in the rest of the letter that many now see this section as not even written by Paul but rather added at a later date, perhaps decades after Paul's death. Although such literary speculations seem to be removed from spirituality, knowing whether or not Paul actually wrote these anti-feminine lines could have enormous practical significance. Some churches today are being torn apart by a blind desire to be loyal to Paul. We will discuss the evidence behind these opposing views when we look at this section.

Paul's Letter Writing

First Corinthians is not Paul's first letter. It is not even his first letter to the Corinthians. He says very clearly at First Corinthians 5:9 that he wrote the Corinthians an earlier letter, which we apparently no longer have—unless a snippet of it was later edited into Second Corinthians 6:14–7:1. Paul's earliest extent letter is First Thessalonians, written probably from Corinth around A.D. 52. If Paul wrote Second Thessalonians, he would have had to write it shortly after his first letter, perhaps within months. We have good reasons, however, for thinking that Second Thessalonians was written by a follower of Paul decades after Paul's death. In that case First Corinthians would be the next letter written some three years later from Ephesus. Second Corinthians, which is almost certainly an edited collection of several letters, would be written during a span of about a year after First Corinthians (A.D. 55–56) as Paul moved from Ephesus to Macedonia. Romans appears to be written from Corinth around A.D. 58. Galatians is difficult to date and locate. Scholars will present different hypotheses. However, its similarity with Romans strongly suggests that Paul wrote this letter in conjunction with Romans, perhaps shortly before finishing Romans.

Philippians, Philemon, and Colossians are very difficult to situate in time and place. Scholars will differ widely as they try to create a chronology of these letters. Many prefer to see Colossians written after Paul's death. In all three letters, Paul describes himself as in prison. Traditionally these "captivity letters" are situated during the Roman imprisonment described in Acts 28:16–31. The theology of Philippians and Colossians suggests a late stage in Paul's career. However, details in Philippians suggest he is not far from Philippi, perhaps in Ephesus. Details in Philemon suggest he is not far from Colossae, perhaps in Ephesus. And Ephesus would be a likely place for Paul to have written Colossians. Placing these "captivity letters" in Ephesus in the mid-sixties is a reasonable hypothesis.

For reasons we cannot develop here, we are going to presuppose that the Letter to the Ephesians along with those to Timothy and to Titus were written after Paul's death by a disciple of Paul, writing in Paul's name. These letters (and perhaps Colossians) belong to a group of writings named "deutero-pauline." They are inspired; they are precious; but they do not reflect Paul's personal theology. They reflect the first interpretations of that theology.

With this overview, we have an ability to situate Paul's statements in First Corinthians in a literary context. We can compare these statements with what Paul has already written. We can compare these with statements Paul will later write. In both comparisons, we can sense both how Paul often changes his views in the course of his lifetime and also how he maintains the same view although expressing it somewhat differently. By comparing Paul's statements with those in the deutero-pauline letters, we can see how the next generation developed Paul's thought and sometimes moved away from ideas which Paul insisted on.

Actualizing First Corinthians

Paul did not write to us. He is responding to questions the Corinthians asked some two thousand years ago from a very different culture. Although we must never forget the letter form in which Paul expresses his truth, there are ways in which we can give Paul's letter a new existence. First of all, we can find in a more generalized form something of our questions in the questions of the Corinthians. We may not want to ask the question about meat offered to idols (cf. 8:1–13), but we hold deep in our hearts the question of living and adapting our faith in a culture basically hostile to our faith. We may not want to ask the question about how the dead body will rise (cf. 15:35–49), but we constantly ask the question of life after death and the way our bodies fit into God's plan of ultimate salvation.

Secondly, when Paul answered the questions of the Corinthians he brought to bear material and ideas that contain more truth than simply answers to those questions. When Paul answered the question about the proper way to celebrate the Lord's Supper, he backs up and writes about the traditions of the Last Supper (11:23–26). He considers what it means to be at table fellowship with the Lord in the church of God (11:20–22). It is through the excess meaning in Paul's answers that Paul's letter to the Corinthians can begin to answer our questions.

First Corinthians is above all a letter written about the church, a church of sinners, but a church which becomes nothing less than the body of Christ. To actualize this letter for our spirituality means to be deeply aware of our real questions about church. Not all of them will be answered or even remotely addressed. But every so often a text of Paul jumps out as intensely meaningful. Somehow one of our questions has been touched.

To be able to identify the "excess" in Paul's answers to Corinth requires knowledge of more than this letter. It requires a gradually growing familiarity with the rest of Paul, with the rest of the New Testament, and with the rest of the Bible. In this expanding view, we begin to see the wealth Paul brings to his questions. The "excess" becomes more evident to those who cultivate a sensitivity to the larger theological picture.

This cultivation is similar to that which allows some people to see great beauty in a work of art. The beauty is real. It is not just in the eye of the beholder, but the eye of the beholder must be trained to see it. Actually, this may be more a training of the heart than of the eye, a heart enlivened by the same spirit in which the work of art was created.

The Spirit guiding Paul is the same Spirit who unites us as we listen to Paul read today in church.

I
Letter Opening
(1:1–9)

As in his other letters, Paul follows the conventions of ancient letter writing.

The Greeting (1:1–3)

Most personal letters began with a very short identification of parties and a greeting, such as "Gaius to his brother, Titus, greetings (*chairein*)." If you were Jewish, your greeting would more likely be "peace" (*shalom*). Paul knows these conventions, but will not pass up an opportunity to express his faith:

> [1]Paul, called to be an apostle of Christ Jesus by the will of God, and Sosthenes our brother, [2]to the church of God that is in Corinth, to you who have been sanctified in Christ Jesus, called to be holy, with all those everywhere who call upon the name of the Lord Jesus Christ, their Lord and ours. [3]Grace to you and peace from God our Father and the Lord Jesus Christ.

Unlike most personal letter writers of his day, Paul consistently adds a description of himself as he introduces himself as the writer. The letter will involve matters of "tough love." Not surprisingly therefore, Paul describes his authority, "an apostle of Christ Jesus." That puts him on a rank with "the Twelve," whom we know from the gospels. He may not have been with Jesus during his public ministry, but he has seen the risen Lord. As he says later in this letter, this experience of Jesus, the risen Lord is what makes him an apostle (9:1). Paul's theocentric faith comes out immediately. He is an apostle by the initiative and plan of God, the Father (cf. Gal 1:15–16). Paul also frequently associates others in his letter writing, a gesture which augments the public character of this writing. Unless Sosthenes is the synagogue leader of Acts 18:17, we do not know anything else about him.

When Paul names his intended readers, he also adapts the letter writing conventions to add significant descriptions. We could develop a theology of church just by looking at these descriptions. The expression "church of God, which is . . ." suggests something larger than the assembly of Christians at Corinth. It suggests a reality which can be present in many places. The church of the Corinthians is not alone, not an isolated group. They share a network with other churches in different cities, all of which could be considered "the church of God." This universal sense of the expression is particularly clear also at 10:32.

At Corinth various groups probably met often separately in diverse homes, where the Lord's Supper could certainly be managed easier. But here Paul is addressing all the Christians of Corinth as this church of God. He is picturing them perhaps as assembled in the house of Gaius, "host of the whole church" (Rom 16:23). It is on the level of the city-wide church that the full spectrum of spiritual gifts could interact, where the Christians could function really as "the body of Christ" (12:1–31).

For Paul, what makes this church or assembly special? They are "sanctified." They are "holy." Paul thus stresses again how this assembly belongs to God. They also "call on the name of our Lord Jesus Christ." A person looks around when you call his or her name. People of the time of Paul saw the name of a deity as a kind of private e-mail address to that person. For Paul the common access to Jesus among Christians is a bond bringing Christians together, "their Lord and ours."

Paul sends greetings, not with the usual Greek word, *chairein* ("greetings"), but with Paul's favorite thought, *charis* ("grace"), the name of the irrational love of God for us. Paul adds the

Jewish greeting, "peace." *Shalom* in Hebrew literally means "having all your debts paid," a marvelous image of salvation.

Paul here sends "grace and peace" from "God, our Father"—an interesting clue into Paul's sense of authority ("God sends his greetings!"). He also adds "and the Lord, Jesus Christ." Paul's theology is theocentric, but Jesus, as Lord, another focal point. We need to watch carefully the relationship between God and Jesus in Paul's theology. Paul will not call Jesus "God" (*theos*). That title is virtually a proper name of the Father. Jesus is "Lord" (*kyrios*). That title is taken from Greek Jewish references to God, but what it means for Paul is not easy to determine.

For reflection. If you were to identify or describe your local church in one sentence, what would you say? How would you describe its network with the church around the world? Would the common element be "those who call on the name of the Lord"? Combing through this opening to the letter, Paul mentions several aspects of what it means to be a church of God. If you were writing to a church and you wanted to do the same, what aspects would you mention? What really makes a church?

The Letter Prayer (1:4–9)

At this point in the opening, most personal letters added a word or two about "remembering you to the gods" or "I pray that you are in good health." A Jewish letter might include a more elaborate prayer blessing God (cf. 2 Mc 1:2–6). Paul here follows his Jewish background:

> [4]I give thanks to my God always on your account for the grace of God bestowed on you in Christ Jesus, [5]that in him you were enriched in every way, with all discourse and all knowledge, [6]as the testimony to Christ was confirmed among you, [7]so that you are not lacking in any spiritual gift as you

wait for the revelation of our Lord Jesus Christ. [8]He will keep you firm to the end, irreproachable on the day of our Lord Jesus [Christ]. [9]God is faithful, and by him you were called to fellowship with his Son, Jesus Christ our Lord.

When Paul adds a prayer it is not the perfunctory prayer wish often found in personal letters of the time. This prayer sounds very much like the words he would address to God on behalf of the Corinthians. He thanks God! Although Paul will have much to say about Corinthian deficiencies, he starts with an upbeat recognition of the incredible love that God has for this church.

He focuses on the Corinthians' "spiritual gifts," particularly the gifts of "discourse" and "knowledge." We will see more of the meaning of these gifts when we read chapters 12–14. Three years earlier, when he wrote to the Thessalonians, he thanked God for that church's faith and love, as he does in most of his letters. Paul makes no mention of the Corinthians' faith and love. This is probably quite deliberate.

As also frequent in his letter prayers, Paul shifts focus to the future, to "the day of our Lord Jesus [Christ]." If the church is the beachhead of God's kingdom, it must be oriented to the fulfillment of that kingdom. The church is an assembly of people who are "waiting," not like sleepy travelers at an over-booked airport, but like space shuttle watchers listening to a countdown, eyes fixed on the horizon. When delays make the waiting difficult, one truth gives strength, "God is faithful."

For reflection. How would Paul address our church? What would he thank God for? If in writing to us he started with a similar stress on his authority , what do you think he would be preparing to say about our church? If you were to identify the special gifts of your church, what would you mention? In this prayer of Paul, do we find any other aspects to add to an understanding of what it takes to be a church?

II
Issues of Church Unity and Order
(1:10–4:21)

Disunity in the Church of Corinth (1:10–17)

Without pussyfooting around Paul jumps into the main problem to be addressed. He gets his information from Cloe's people, a delegation from a prominent Christian household. He tries a little bit of ridicule and then fumbles around a bit:

> [10]I urge you, brothers, in the name of our Lord Jesus Christ, that all of you agree in what you say, and that there be no divisions among you, but that you be united in the same mind and in the same purpose. [11]For it has been reported to me about you, my brothers, by Cloe's people, that there are rivalries among you. [12]I mean that each of you is saying, "I belong to Paul," or "I belong to Apollos," or "I belong to Kephas." "I belong to Christ."
>
> [13]Is Christ divided? Was Paul crucified for you? Or were you baptized in the name of Paul? [14]I give thanks (to God) that I baptized none of you except Crispus and Gaius, [15]so that no one can say you were baptized in my name. [16](I baptized the household of Stephanas also; beyond that I do not know whether I baptized anyone else.) [17]For Christ did not send me to baptize but to preach the gospel, and not with the wisdom of human eloquence, so that the cross of Christ might not be emptied of its meaning.

The rivalries or factions within the church of Corinth seem to be based on adherence to church leaders rather than on any issue of doctrine or discipline. This was a time, of course, when one's personal relationship generally made you a member of the church, just as the apostles were defined by their personal relationship with Jesus. "Apollos" is mentioned in Acts 18:24–28 as a Jewish follower of John the Baptist, who was quite a theologian with a deep sense of mission. Priscilla and Aquila catechized him in Christianity and apparently introduced him to the Corinthian church. "Cephas" is Peter, Simon bar Jonah. *Kepha* is the Aramaic word Jesus apparently used to designate Simon as *Petros*, the rock (cf. Mt 16:18). Could Peter have worked in Corinth? Are these "Petrine" Christians migratory Christians? More likely, the reference to Peter here is an attempt of Paul simply to widen the perspective. At Corinth it seems the Paul/Apollos division was the one that was doing damage (cf. 3:4; 4:6). It is just as stupid for Christians elsewhere under the leadership of Peter to define themselves primarily by that personal relationship. Paul basically ridicules the idea that the church could be divided according to such human adherence. The line "I belong to Christ" (1:12) must be read as Paul's sarcastic comeback. (The New American Bible [NAB], which I am quoting from in this spiritual commentary, misses this point by connecting it to the preceding by the word "or," which is not in the Greek.) After the homily that Paul is about to insert (cf. introduction), Paul returns to the list of human leaders mentioning "Paul," "Apollos," and "Kephas" (3:21) and then clearly says "And you [belong] to Christ!" (3:22). He should have no problem with the slogan, "I belong to Christ."

Paul's thought then drifts a bit until he sees the need to introduce the homily on true spiritual wisdom. Crispus is probably the converted synagogue leader mentioned in Acts 18:8. Gaius will send greetings from Corinth in Paul's letter to the Romans (Rom 16:23). As host of the whole Corinthian church, Gaius must have had a very large dining room. Stephanas and his household function with some authority role in the Corinthian church (cf. 16:15–17).

By the time he wrote what we have labeled verse 17, Paul realized he must go deeper than simply admonish the Corinthians about conduct. The real problem lay in their lack of understanding of the role of the cross, and he will tie this lack of understanding in with the Corinthians' enthusiasm for the Spirit.

For reflection. Are the divisions in Christianity today at all like the divisions Paul found in Corinth? Sometimes Christians feel quite superior to others because of their link to a particular human leader—like the pope or Martin Luther. But Paul responds, "Is Christ divided?" Notice already Paul is hinting at an identification of the body of Christians with the person of Christ. As we intensify our common "belonging to Christ," we should overcome these divisions.

The Wisdom of the Spirit—God's Folly in the Cross (1:18–25)

Rabbinic homilies were composed for meditation on the synagogue readings. The faithful loved to hear a long string of biblical texts that could be linked together by key words and thus show the unity of God's plan throughout scripture. Paul was well trained in the technique.

[18]The message of the cross is foolishness to those who are perishing, but to us who are being saved it is the power of God. [19]For it is written:

"I will destroy the wisdom of the wise, and the learning of the learned I will set aside." [20]Where is the wise one? Where is the scribe? Where is the debater of this age? Has not God made the wisdom of the world foolish? [21]For since in the wisdom of God the world did not come to know God through wisdom, it was the will of God through the foolishness of the proclamation to save those who have faith. [22]For Jews demand signs and Greeks look for wisdom, [23]but we proclaim Christ crucified, a stumbling block to Jews and foolishness to Gentiles, [24]but to those who are called, Jews and Greeks alike, Christ the power of God and the wisdom of God. [25]For the foolishness of God is wiser than human wisdom, and the weakness of God is stronger than human strength.

Paul's apocalyptic dualism leads him to describe two categories of people, "those who are perishing" and "those being saved." Rarely does Paul speak of a group or of anyone, in effect, suffering some ultimate destruction (cf. also 3:17; 6:9;15:50; Gal 5:21). And while here in this text he seems to add some sort of criteria by which this group can be recognized, Paul never really puts anybody in this group. The concept of "perishing" is very important—and he is referring to an eschatological disaster. It describes our radical capacity to destroy ourselves. It speaks of the seriousness of sin. But when we read what Paul says about God's love and power to save, we can wonder if Paul really thought anyone really was "perishing."

In any case the first criterion that distinguishes the two groups is the ability to understand "the message of the cross." The message of a crucified messiah just does not compute—in human understanding. Paul describes the matrix of this error message as "the wisdom of the world" (1:20). Again Paul draws on Jewish apocalyptic imagery, in which God created not one world but two, this world and the world to come. "This world" has been corrupted by human sin to the extent that it needs to be destroyed and replaced (cf. Rv 21:1).

This description of human inadequacy to understand the plan of God ties into a ancient theme found in both the prophets and in wisdom literature:

For my thoughts are not your thoughts, nor are your ways my ways, says the Lord.
As high as the heavens are above the earth so high are my ways above your ways and my thoughts above your thoughts. (Is 55:8–9)

There is no wisdom, no understanding, no counsel, against the Lord. (Prv 21:20)

Paul here ties into that theme by citing Is 29:14 (1:19) and by alluding to Job 12:17 among other texts (1:20).

By tying into this Old Testament theme Paul says in effect that God's wisdom in this world looks like folly. God's power in this world looks like weakness. The old categorization of people into Jew and Gentile (Greek) does not mean much. Both are fooled by the great lie of this world. The important categorization, the one mentioned at the beginning of the homily, cuts across the division of humanity into Jew and Gentile. Paul here gives a synonym for "those who are being saved." He calls them "those who are called" (1:24). These people are able to stand the world on its head and see the power of God in what appears as weakness and find the wisdom of God in what appears to be folly.

For reflection. The apocalyptic view of "this world" is very pessimistic and is not the only view in the New Testament. Is there any use of this apocalyptic view for Christians today? Can you think of examples where the power and wisdom of God today might be appearing in "weak" and "stupid" people? How could a focus on the crucifixion of Jesus affect the way we might run a small business today? Could we work with this focus in a big corporation?

Paul contrasts God's wisdom with human wisdom. What aspects of God's wisdom appears as foolishness in this world? Why does it appear foolish? Can you think of an experience in your life, when God's way did not make any sense to you at all?

The Wisdom of the Spirit—The Example of the Christians Themselves (1:26–31)

Paul's development of his theme is by way of examples. The first example he gives is the very church he is addressing:

> [26]Consider your own calling, brothers. Not many of you were wise by human standards, not many were powerful, not

many were of noble birth. [27]Rather, God chose the foolish of the world to shame the wise, and God chose the weak of the world to shame the strong, [28]and God chose the lowly and despised of the world, those who count for nothing, to reduce to nothing those who are something, [29]so that no human being might boast before God. [30]It is due to him that you are in Christ Jesus, who became for us wisdom from God, as well as righteousness, sanctification, and redemption, [31]so that as it is written, "Whoever boasts, should boast in the Lord."

Although some in the Corinthian congregation would fit the categories described by Paul here, the "low class" Christians he seems to be addressing could have been a very different group—given our hypothesis that this homily was thought out and composed before the letter. As a matter of fact we see many rather wealthy people in Corinth. They are referred to by Paul in this letter (1:11; 16:15–18) and by other New Testament writings (Acts 18:2–3.7; Rom 16:23).

Using the word "calling" (1:26; cf. 1:24) as a hinge, Paul develops his theme of the apocalyptic reversal of values by drawing attention to the quality of God's chosen people. By definition, by nature these are "the poor of Yahweh." The contrast between most of the Christian gatherings and the splendor of Roman assemblies, the contrast between the simple Lord's supper and the glorious feasts of political heros must have tested the faith of anyone asking where was history being made in God's eyes. "To be somebody" was very important in the days of Paul. To be strong, to be noble meant the difference between security and respect on the one hand and constant danger and social ridicule on the other.

Paul concludes and links the section to his homily with a very free citation of Jeremiah which actually reads:

Thus says the Lord: Let not the wise man glory in his wisdom, nor the strong man glory in his strength, nor the rich man glory in his riches;

But rather, let him who glories, glory in this, that in his
    prudence he knows me. (Jer 9:22–23)

The first part of this citation seems to have guided Paul in his
rhetorical listing of great ones of this world who are to be
shamed by God's lowly.

For reflection. As little children we are programed to pursue a
career that will bring wealth and respect. We become
workaholics in this pursuit. And the momentum of this pursuit
sometimes carries us roughshod over ethical values. Does Paul's
apocalyptic perspective address this education? Where do we
find a church that clearly looks like "the poor of Yahweh"?

The Wisdom of the Spirit—The Example of Paul (2:1–5)

The next five verses, which describe Paul himself as an
example of God's apocalyptic reversal of values, may have been
part of the original homily or may have been added as an adaption
to the Corinthians. It is the one section that does not
contain a Scriptural allusion or citation.

> [1]When I came to you, brothers, proclaiming the mystery of
> God, I did not come with sublimity of words or of wisdom.
> [2]For I resolved to know nothing while I was with you except
> Jesus Christ, and him crucified. [3]I came to you in weakness
> and fear and much trembling, [4]and my message and my proc-
> lamation were not with persuasive [words of] wisdom, but
> with a demonstration of spirit and power, [5]so that your faith
> might rest not on human wisdom but on the power of God.

Unlike the portrayal of Paul in Acts (cf. Acts 14:11–13),
Paul's self image is rather humble (cf. also Gal 4:13–14). Of
course, the lines here are ironic. This paragraph along with this
whole homily shows a mastery of rhetoric and good
writing—according to the standards of Paul's day. Perhaps Paul
refers only to his oral preaching. The point, however, is clear.

Not only is the content of the gospel a matter of human folly, but the medium of this message carries the same mark of Christ's crucifixion.

Hence the "demonstration of Spirit and power" (The NAB chooses not to capitalize "spirit") probably does not refer to anything miraculous. Such an interpretation would contradict everything Paul has been saying about the human demand for signs (1:22–23). In fact Paul asserted that the "power of God" is nothing other than "the word of the cross" (1:18). The expression "spirit and power" appears to be a dual expression for one thing (a hendiadys), hence the same as "the powerful Spirit." And Paul is about to explain how the Spirit of God provides wisdom and insight to those who love God.

The Wisdom of the Spirit—Wisdom for the Mature (2:6–9)

The section from 1:18 to 2:5 has been rather negative, insisting on the difference between the wisdom and divine wisdom. Now Paul adds the positive side. This divine wisdom is accessible to human beings:

> [6]Yet we do speak a wisdom to those who are mature, but not a wisdom of this age, or of the rulers of this age who are passing away. [7]Rather, we speak God's wisdom, mysterious, hidden, which God predetermined before the ages for our glory, [8]and which none of the rulers of this age knew for, if they had known it, they would not have crucified the Lord of glory. [9]But as it is written:
> "What eye has not seen, and ear has not heard,
> and what has not entered the human heart,
> what God has prepared for those who love him."

Again we see the apocalyptic dualism of Paul, on the one hand, "this age" and "the rulers of this age"; on the other hand, "the mature" or "those who love God." Paul speaks of a "wisdom in mystery" that is available for the second group, but not for the first group. The crucifixion here is the mark of the inaccessibility of this wisdom for the rulers or princes of this age. Paul appears to be using the term "mature" (*teleios*) as a designation for Christians. The word can also be translated "perfect," but the sense here is apocalyptic rather than ethical. Paul is not talking about a class of people who by some ethical effort have refined their person to perfection, but rather of a group who by their new being in faith begin to live the life of the End (*telos*). This is the meaning of the term as found in the gospels (cf. Mt 19:21).

When Paul later writes of the great mystery hidden in past ages, now revealed to his holy ones, he refers to nothing other than the gospel itself (Rom 16:25–27; Col 1:26–27). To describe the contents of this wisdom in mystery, Paul here cites Isaiah 64:3, an Old Testament text which refers to God's salvation in history. Thus Paul is probably not referring to eschatological realities but to the grace already bestowed on the world through the crucifixion.

For reflection. Did you ever wonder why God hides himself and his plans so much? If God's plans are so important, why does he not blare them from heaven in an unmistakable way for all to understand? What does it really take to hear the word of God and understand God's message?

The Wisdom of the Spirit—Revelation through the Spirit (2:10–16)

Paul now describes the role of the Spirit of God in acquisition of this wisdom which allows the believer to see in the crucifixion the wisdom and power of God:

> [10]This God has revealed to us through the Spirit. For the Spirit scrutinizes everything, even the depths of God. [11]Among human beings who knows what pertains to a person except the spirit of the person that is within? Similarly, no

one knows what pertains to God except the Spirit of God. [12]We have not received the spirit of the world but the Spirit that is from God, so that we may understand the gifts freely given us by God. [13]And we speak about them not with words taught by human wisdom, but with words taught by the Spirit, describing spiritual realities in spiritual terms.

[14]Now the natural [*psychikos*] person does not accept what pertains to the Spirit of God, for to him it is foolishness, and he cannot understand it, because it is judged spiritually. [15]The spiritual [*pneumatikos*] person, however, can judge everything but is not subject to judgment by anyone.

[16]For "who has known the mind of the Lord, so as to counsel him?" But we have the mind of Christ.

By comparing the Spirit of God with the spirit of a human being, both in relationship to the knowledge (the "scrutinizing") of each, Paul gives us a precious insight into his understanding of the Spirit of God and the connection between wisdom and the Spirit. Paul actually makes a triple comparison:

- The spirit of a human being→the [depths] of a person (2:11a)

- The Spirit of God→ the depths of God (2:10 and 11b)

- The Spirit from God→the gifts from God (2:12).

While in the original Greek verse 11 does not contain the words "the depths" but simply the article "the . . ." without a corresponding noun, the perfect agreement in number and gender of the article with "the depths" in verse 10, strongly suggests Paul is elliptically referring to "the depths," rather than the very general "what pertains to a person" which the NAB uses in its translation shown here.

The first element of the comparison describes the ability limited to a person's inner consciousness to know what is in one's own heart. This view is not just a modern position. In the collection of "Solomon's proverbs" we find: "A lamp from the

Lord is the breath of man, it searches through all his inmost being" (Prv 20:27). The view of how inscrutable is the human heart to an outsider is also often expressed. The modern philosopher would speak about this knowledge as a presence, the lived contact of immediate consciousness. Such philosophical refinement is out of place either in Paul or in Proverbs, but the idea is there. Thus when the comparison moves to the Spirit of God and knowing the depths of God, again we get a sense that the Spirit of God is basically God's inner life, God's consciousness of who and what God is. The third comparison connects with the topic at hand. God shares his Spirit. God shares his breath or life. The result is our ability to understand "the gifts from God." Just as "the Spirit from God" is more external than "the Spirit of God," so "the gifts of God" is more external than "the depths of God," although both external manifestations are rooted in the internal life of God.

What knowledge is Paul talking about? What is this "wisdom in mystery for the mature"? From the above comparison, this knowledge appears now more as a lived experience of God's grace. It means a kind of "attunement" to the wavelength of God, possible by a sharing in the very self-consciousness of God. Thus this knowledge results from and entails a transformation of being. The "mature" person is the "spiritual" (*pneumatikos*) person.

If we connect this part of the homily with the first half, we see that Paul is describing the way in which the great gift of God, the crucifixion, will appear as weakness and folly to the unspiritual, to the person of this age. Only the gift of the Spirit, which lifts us to the "foolish" life of God can give us a sense of the crucifixion as power and wisdom. This gift is equivalent to having "the mind of Christ," as Paul ends this section with a free citation of Isaiah 40:13.

For reflection. The thoughts are breathtaking. Paul has not only cited the prophets and the sages of Israel, he has grasped and applied their basic insight into the Spirit of prophecy and wisdom. He confronts us with the paradox and mystery of God, the ultimate otherness of God—where power is weakness and folly is wisdom. The chasm between "God's world" and "this world" gapes in front of us. How can we leap into such darkness? The crucifixion says it all. This is the entry point of the divine into this world, and this is our entry point to the divine world. What a horror! Yet what a gift! Only the very Spirit of God can sustain us in the presence of this mystery.

The Spirit which Paul describes is not one that comes in fire and wind, but rather inhabits the heart in a subtle and interior mode. Like the immediate presence we have of ourselves, this Spirit might not be at all evident until we stop and reflect and thus catch only a passing glimpse. Yet for Paul this Spirit allows the gifts of God to resonate in our hearts. How then do we experience the Spirit? What are the manifestations of this Spirit?

Application to the Corinthian Church (3:1–4)

At this point Paul breaks away from his homily on wisdom and the Spirit to apply this message to the Corinthians. The topic returns to that of church unity:

> [1]Brothers, I could not talk to you as spiritual people, but as fleshly people, as infants in Christ. [2]I fed you milk, not solid food, because you were unable to take it. Indeed, you are still not able, even now, [3]for you are still of the flesh. While there is jealousy and rivalry among you, are you not of the flesh and behaving in an ordinary human way? [4]Whenever someone says, "I belong to Paul," and another, "I belong to Apollos," are you not merely human?

Up to this point Paul has relied on his apocalyptic dualism to describe two categories of people, those being saved, i.e., the spiritual, and those perishing, i.e., the unspiritual. Now he turns to the Corinthians—the church so proud of its spiritual gifts—and says that he cannot speak to them as spiritual people.

In the dualistic view, such a description would practically identify the Corinthians as those perishing.

Actually Paul backs away from that identification and instead adds a third category, "fleshy people" or "infants in Christ." The sudden and unexplained shift from the dualism of the homily suggests sarcasm on the part of Paul. "Fleshy Christians" are not normal. Such an idea belongs to the category of paradox. Yes, they are Christians; they are "in Christ." But they seem to lack an essential of Christian life—the presence of the Spirit. This combination for Paul would be a paradox.

This status thus invented here by Paul is something like that of those beginning faith, like "infants" (*nepioi*). Describing someone as an "infant" is not a compliment for Paul—despite what Jesus said (cf. Mt 11:25; 21:26; Lk 10:21). Paul uses the expression "the infant" as the contrast to "the mature" (2:6), the person capable of understanding God's wisdom and gifts. It would have been a bitter pill to swallow for the Corinthians to hear this description of themselves.

Yet Paul is adamant. If love is lacking from the community, that community is not Spirit-filled. He does not care how many other spectacular spiritual manifestations mark a church. Without love and the consequent sense of unity, that community is dangerously close to "those who are perishing."

For reflection. What would Paul say about the quality of our parish or community, about the spiritual life of our family? If he were looking for a level of love and unity, what manifestations could he observe? What else might he be looking for? If we were creating an instrument for measuring the spiritual life of a faith community, would we place the same emphasis on unity? What else would we think is important?

Ministry in the Church (3:5–17)

Since the Corinthian problem seems to be some special attachment to a spiritual leader, in this case either Paul or

Apollos, Paul writes his thoughts about the role of ministry in the church:

> [5]What is Apollos, after all, and what is Paul? Ministers through whom you became believers, just as the Lord assigned each one. [6]I planted, Apollos watered, but God caused the growth. [7]Therefore neither the one who plants nor the one who waters is anything, but only God, who causes the growth. [8]The one who plants and the one who waters are equal, and each will receive wages in proportion to his labor. [9]For we are God's co-workers; you are God's field, God's building.
>
> [10]According to the grace of God given to me, like a wise master builder I laid a foundation, and another is building upon it. But each one must be careful how he builds upon it, [11]for no one can lay a foundation other than the one that is there, namely, Jesus Christ. [12]If anyone builds on this foundation with gold, silver, precious stones, wood, hay, or straw, [13]the work of each will come to light, for the Day will disclose it. It will be revealed with fire, and the fire [itself] will test the quality of each one's work. [14]If the work stands that someone built upon the foundation, that person will receive a wage. [15]But if someone's work is burned up, that one will suffer loss; the person will be saved, but only as through fire. [16]Do you not know that you are the temple of God, and that the Spirit of God dwells in you? [17]If anyone destroys God's temple, God will destroy that person; for the temple of God, which you are, is holy.

Mixing the images of a farm (3:5–9) with that of a construction site (3:6–17), Paul reflects on the process of building up the Christian community, which is nothing less than God's temple. Paul wants to describe the seriousness of ministry within that community, yet he starts by pointing out the relative unimportance of identifying which human minister is doing what. Somebody has to plant and somebody has to water, but to make a big deal of who does what on this level is to forget that the primary activity is God's. Paul repeats the same idea with construction imagery. Here the primary role—compared to which everybody else's activity is secondary—is that of Jesus Christ, described as the foundation of the church.

Running through these descriptions are several images of ministry. Paul sees himself as "God's co-worker" for God's field (3:9), as a "wise master builder" for God's temple (3:10).

Drawing on one of the early Christians' favorite Old Testament books, the Book of Daniel, Paul lists a series of materials given in descending order of "value," some of which is combustible and others not (3:12). The imagery now allows Paul to consider the possibility that some ministerial contributions might be "junk." Paul is confident that God can handle this situation by an eschatological, that is end of times, purification. At the same time Paul insists on the responsibility of the minister, who will either "receive a wage" or "suffer loss" depending on the quality of his or her ministry.

The church of Corinth is a very special building, the Temple of God. The Spirit of God dwells in that church. Describing the presence of the Spirit, the imagery here is collective, whereas the imagery in the preceding homily seemed more individual, as it will when Paul in later writings describes the Spirit dwelling in our hearts (Gal 4:6; Rom 8:9, 15).

Suddenly the image of 587 B.C. flashes into Paul's mind, the year the Babylonian army under king Nebuchadnezzar destroyed the Temple of Jerusalem. There are no guarantees. The Temple of God can be destroyed. Ministry in and for that Temple is very serious.

For reflection. Can Paul reasonably say two things at once: ministry is a very serious matter both for the minister and for the church, and ministry is not that important compared to God or Christ's role in the effort? Should we get upset if we do not like the manner of ministerial leadership in our church? What is my ministry in the church, is it precious or is it combustible junk?

It is interesting how Paul in effect reminds us of the trinitarian aspect in our ecclesiology: *God* gives growth, *Jesus* is the foundation, the *Spirit of God* dwells in us as a community. These are three images, each one associated with a "person of the Trinity" as we would say today. From these images alone, how would you describe the role of each divine person?

The Wisdom of the Spirit—Conclusion (3:18–23)

At this point in his letter, Paul remembers he has interrupted his old homily and decides to give the concluding thoughts of that homily, the part that ends with "double whammy" biblical citations that congregations loved to hear at the end of a rabbinic homily:

> [18]Let no one deceive himself. If anyone among you considers himself wise in this age, let him become a fool so as to become wise. [19]For the wisdom of this world is foolishness in the eyes of God, for it is written:
>
> "He catches the wise in their own ruses,"
>
> [20]and again:
>
> "The Lord knows the thoughts of the wise,
> that they are vain."
>
> [21]So let no one boast about human beings, for everything belongs to you, [22]Paul or Apollos or Kephas, or the world or life or death, or the present or the future: all belong to you, [23]and you to Christ, and Christ to God.

We are back in the apocalyptic world of the homily (see above) where black is white, up is down, and foolishness is wisdom—all because "this age/world" is not God's age to come. The two citations, from Job 5:13 and Psalm 94:11 are great examples from wisdom literature of the Old Testament. Wisdom is obviously something to be pursued and treasured, but wisdom is paradoxical. True wisdom comes to human beings enshrouded with the mystery of God—as Job had to acknowledge.

Paul alludes to the great mysteries of life and death, the present and the future, mysteries that can perplex and discourage us, but with which we can live in love. They are all part of God's loving gifts to us however mysterious. With these allusions Paul ties in the original issues begun way back at 1:12, namely, attitudes towards church leadership. Not that "Paul, Apollos" or "Kephas" really belong to us, but Paul brings in these names for the sake of getting back to the problems in Corinth. Again the awkwardness of the expression here suggests the names are added by Paul at this time to the preexisting conclusion of the homily.

For reflection. Paul deals with the ethical problem of church rivalries and factionalism by going deeper to a theological level. Paul is not a moralist, one who simply names action to avoid or pursue. Moralism leads to legalism ("Do it just because you are supposed to do it"). Paul here coaches us to resolve an ethical or moral issue by understanding how God functions in our lives. Paul asks us to look at God, at Jesus, and at the Holy Spirit. It is in that view that we will gain insight into the conduct to which we are called.

More on Paul's Ministry (4:1–21)

The lines that follow clearly continue the thought line of 3:17 and have an even tighter link back to 3:9 continuing the images of Paul's ministry:

> [1]Thus should one regard us: as servants of Christ and stewards of the mysteries of God. [2]Now it is of course required of stewards that they be found trustworthy. [3]It does not concern me in the least that I be judged by you or any human tribunal; I do not even pass judgment on myself; [4]I am not conscious of anything against me, but I do not thereby stand acquitted;

the one who judges me is the Lord. ⁵Therefore, do not make any judgment before the appointed time, until the Lord comes, for he will bring to light what is hidden in darkness and will manifest the motives of our hearts, and then everyone will receive praise from God.

⁶I have applied these things to myself and Apollos for your benefit, brothers, so that you may learn from us not to go beyond what is written, so that none of you will be inflated with pride in favor of one person over another. ⁷Who confers distinction upon you? What do you possess that you have not received? But if you have received it, why are you boasting as if you did not receive it? ⁸You are already satisfied; you have already grown rich; you have become kings without us! Indeed, I wish that you had becomes kings, so that we also might become kings with you.

⁹For as I see it, God has exhibited us apostles as the last of all, like people sentenced to death, since we have become a spectacle to the world, to angels and human beings alike. ¹⁰We are fools on Christ's account, but you are wise in Christ; we are weak, but you are strong; you are held in honor, but we in disrepute. ¹¹To this very hour we go hungry and thirsty, we are poorly clad and roughly treated, we wander about homeless ¹²and we toil, working with our own hands. When ridiculed, we bless; when persecuted, we endure; ¹³when slandered, we respond gently. We have become like the world's rubbish, the scum of all, to this very moment.

¹⁴I am writing you this not to shame you, but to admonish you as my beloved children. ¹⁵Even if you should have countless guides to Christ, yet you do not have many fathers, for I became your father in Christ Jesus through the gospel. ¹⁶Therefore, I urge you, be imitators of me. ¹⁷For this reason I am sending you Timothy, who is my beloved and faithful son in the Lord; he will remind you of my ways in Christ [Jesus], just as I teach them everywhere in every church.

¹⁸Some have become inflated with pride, as if I were not coming to you. ¹⁹But I will come to you soon, if the Lord is willing, and I shall ascertain not the talk of these inflated people but their power. ²⁰For the kingdom of God is not a

matter of talk but of power. [21]Which do you prefer? Shall I come to you with a rod, or with love and a gentle spirit?

Tough talk! The section is filled with sarcasm. "You people don't need me, you have it all!" When Paul describes the Corinthians as "wise" in the way he himself is a "fool," "strong" in the way he is "weak," "held in honor" in the way he is lives in "disrepute" (4:10), we hear echoes of the homily on wisdom. The apocalyptic chasm that separates this age from the next and reverses the appearance of values—this chasm suggests that the Corinthians are in big trouble. The sufferings and humiliations of Paul (4:11–13) are far better indications of belonging to the age to come (4:5). Being "well seen," being in "a position of power," having an office "of honor"—even in the church—is not a good sign. In his own eyes, Paul is anything but a high ranking official. Paul thus becomes a model to imitate (4:16).

The world of Paul at this time was built up around "honor." When you met someone on the street or down in the market place, the first thing you were supposed to do is figure out if that person were "more honorable" than you or not. Your interaction with that person was then determined by that judgment. Paul knew about this. Everything we know about him suggests he was well-bred, coming from a family that could afford the education he obviously had. But he saw in Christ the total reversal of this social system. On the other hand, nothing indicates that Paul wanted to change this social system. He does not seem to have a revolutionary bone in his body—at least as far as politics and society go. But he sees through this social order as a sham. It belongs to "this world" which is passing away. What really seems to irritate Paul, however, is to see these "worldly" values infiltrate the church of Christ. He really does look irritated at the Corinthians in this passage.

Paul's admonition not "to make any judgment" on people before the day of judgment (4:5) is not terribly consistent with his instructions to follow about sinners in the church (cf. 5:1–13). It is interesting, nevertheless, how Paul focuses only on the positive side of this day of judgment. He speaks only of people receiving "praise from God" (4:5). He never speaks of people receiving a condemnation from God.

If Paul grew up in a world where honor and position seemed to be keys to happiness, he would be interested in praise. As a young man he probably had many deep ambitions. Now he sees how those ambitions could be part of the great paradox of the cross. His praise and honor is from God, not from human beings.

As Paul provides more images of his ministry—"servant (*hypertes*) of Christ" (4:1), "steward (*oikonomos*) of the mysteries of God" (4:1), "your father (*pater*) in Christ Jesus" (4:15)—he adds more colors and traits to the overall picture of Christian ministry. For one thing, by the choice of words he suggests that such ministry is a situation of intense accountability. The word he uses for "servant" frequently describes an assistant to a king or other powerful person. The word "steward" describes a person who has full control of another's household assets. In both descriptions the role is defined by the relationship to a more important person, to whom the assistant and steward must frequently give an account (cf. the story in Lk 19:11–27). Paul alludes to that accountability by describing himself as "trustworthy" (*pistos*). This is a description of a person who is firm or solid like a great boulder. The language is rooted in the Hebrew concept *'aman*, the word that describes God as the trustworthy rock for the Israelites (Dt 32:4), and the word we use to end a prayer, "Amen." It is as if we say, "It is sure!" In situations where Paul could have been deeply discouraged and tempted to give up his ministry (vv. 11–13), he remains solid.

Furthermore, his description of himself as "father" to the Corinthians implies a bond far stronger than that of some specific functional relationship. Paul describes himself as a "father" of communities or disciples many times (Phil 2:22; 1 Thes 2:11). Once he described himself as a "nursing mother" (1 Thes 2:7). Nothing in his writings suggests that Paul had children, but he seems to know the almost limitless obligations of a parent. You simply cannot walk away when things go bad. You must "go bad" with your children. You suffer everything they suffer, and you rejoice in everything they rejoice about. A loving parent's anger at a child—like Paul's anger in this text—often reflects the maddening fact that the parent must carry in his or her heart the child's stupidity and mistakes.

For reflection. Ministry in the church is no trivial matter. Ministers should not carry the trappings of power and authority which this world understands. Paul exemplifies the absences of these trappings. But Christian ministers carry the power of the kingdom of God—the power that looks like weakness in this world. Paul exemplifies this power. It is the power and authority of a loving parent. Parents—especially parents of teen-agers—know the feeling of powerlessness. There are no worldly trappings here. Yet a child's life is in their hands. It is the power and authority of love. Sometimes tough love. Paul threatens to come with a rod (4:21). But Paul sees himself as "your father in Christ Jesus through the gospel" (4:15).

III

Major Moral Disorders
(5:1—6:14)

Paul turns now to the reports from the delegations (see Introduction) about three special situations which he apparently saw as serious immorality, a case of incest at Corinth, public lawsuits involving Christians, and general sexual license. Here we tune in to the earliest recorded recognition by a church that it is in fact a church of sinners.

A Case of Incest (5:1–12)

[1]It is widely reported that there is immorality among you, and immorality of a kind not found even among pagans—a man living with his father's wife. [2]And you are inflated with pride. Should you not rather have been sorrowful? The one who did this deed should be expelled from your midst. [3]I, for my part, although absent in body but present in spirit, have already, as if present, pronounced judgment on the one who has committed this deed, [4]in the name of [our] Lord Jesus: when you have gathered together and I am with you in spirit with the power of the Lord Jesus, [5]you are to deliver this man to Satan for the destruction of his flesh, so that his spirit may be saved on the day of the Lord.

[6]Your boasting is not appropriate. Do you not know that a little yeast leavens all the dough? [7]Clear out the old yeast, so that you may become a fresh batch of dough, inasmuch as you are unleavened. For our paschal lamb, Christ, has been sacrificed. [8]Therefore, let us celebrate the feast, not with the old yeast, the yeast of malice and wickedness, but with the unleavened bread of sincerity and truth.

⁹I wrote you in my letter not to associate with immoral people, ¹⁰not at all referring to the immoral of this world or the greedy and robbers or idolaters; for you would then have to leave the world. ¹¹But I now write to you not to associate with anyone named a brother, if he is immoral, greedy, an idolater, a slanderer, a drunkard, or a robber, not even to eat with such a person. ¹²For why should I be judging outsiders? Is it not your business to judge those within? ¹³God will judge those outside. "Purge the evil person from your midst."

When we read this angry response of Paul telling the community to expel from the community the one committing incest, we think of Jesus pardoning the adulteress (Jn 8:1–11) or the Pharisees upset by Jesus eating with sinners (Mk 2:16–17). In fact we are perplexed by the Paul's instruction "to judge those within" the community (5:12) when he had just written "do not make any judgment before the appointed time" (4:5). Maybe this inconsistency is an example of how letters are not to be read as systematic essays (see Introduction).

The aspect of this admonition that does make sense, however, is Paul's anger at the community for their apparent approval of the sin, their being "inflated" by the event, as Paul says. He uses the same expression later regarding some form of "knowledge" contrasted with "love" (8:1). Paul perceives the community at Corinth kicking back and winking at the incest in the thought that their spiritual level makes such sexual matters trivial. He is really angry at the community, perhaps at the community leadership, for not taking control of the situation and fulfilling their obligation of fraternal correction—as Jesus had commanded as described in Matthew 18:15–20. In fact the Matthian instruction about "the church"—dealing with the member sinner, gathering in the name of Jesus, supported by the spiritual presence of Jesus, with the power to bind and loose—sounds very much like Paul's instruction to the Corinthians to gather for this disciplinary action (5:4). Both texts reflect the growing sense of the church that "the holy ones" are not always so holy after all, and that we simply must find a way to deal with sinfulness within.

Whatever "delivering to Satan" (5:5) meant to Paul, it clearly does not mean consigning to hell. Paul instead refers to some type of destruction of the person's "flesh" and the salvation of his "spirit," indicating some medicinal punishment. In later writings, the "flesh/spirit" antithesis will clearly refer to apocalyptic duality of "this world/the world to come" (cf. Gal 5:16–26; Rom 8:1–13). Juxtaposing the images of "destruction of the flesh" with "saving the spirit" sounds much like "death/resurrection" motif which underpins Paul's basic sense of redemption (cf. Rom 8:3–4).

The reference to the combined feasts of Unleavened Bread and Passover (5:6–8; cf. Ex 12:1–28) may be a part of a recent homily Paul had given. (As I stated in the introduction, he is writing shortly after the feast of Passover.) Although Paul thinks primarily of sin in apocalyptic terms—as a cosmic force—he is clearly concerned about sin as an ethical matter, as expressed in human conduct. The old yeast represents our "malice and wickedness," which becomes our responsibility.

The brief reference, "Our paschal lamb, Christ, has been sacrificed" (5:7) is the earliest written attempt of Paul to say how the death of Jesus can make sense as saving. In itself, the death of Jesus was civil act, that is an execution of a condemned convict. Just the same it was an ugly, horrible act. What Paul is doing here is finding an interpretive image by which this horrible act can be understood as saving. He finds this image in the sacrificial system of the temple—also rather ugly from several standpoints. At the time of Paul the slaughtering of the paschal lamb was seen as a sacrifice. In this bloody sacrificial system, Paul found a way of imaging death as life-giving.

The "letter" mentioned at 5:9 along with a brief description of its contents show that First Corinthians is not Paul's first letter to the Corinthians. We may have completely lost this letter, or it may be present in a "lumpy" section of Second Corinthians (cf. 6:14–7:1). Paul's reflections on this earlier letter bring to mind two things: first, Christians must live in a culture basically hostile to their faith and somehow adjust to that culture; secondly, that culture should not be the norm for the life of the community. When dealing with vice or virtue, Paul likes lists. Lists were a characteristic of the contemporary Stoic philosophers whose literary style is frequently reflected in Paul's letters. The list of vices at 5:11 is similar to the list coming up at 6:9.

For reflection. How are we to live in a culture that is basically hostile to our faith? With some elements we come to terms. Yet Paul indicates a line over which we should not pass. The Christian community should reflect the Kingdom, not the modern world. The issue here is that of "association." Jesus associated with sinners because he was godly. Paul is worried about an association where the norms of the worldly infiltrate into the community. To the extent we are godly, there is no real problem. To the extent we are sinners, we have a problem.

In his *letter*, Paul urges something like "excommunication." Maybe that was what was needed in this concrete circumstance—which *letters* are meant to address (see Introduction). Maybe Paul was wrong here in terms of the need to excommunicate the sinner. We are dealing with a very ambiguous situation. The issue, however, of tacit approval is clear. The community must take a stand against sinful behavior. But the issue of pastoral care of the individual sinner is by no means settled by this letter.

Lawsuits before Unbelievers (6:1–11)

Paul now turns to a second major ethical issue at Corinth, the practice of suing fellow Christians in the civil courts:

> [1]How can any one of you with a case against another dare to bring it to the unjust for judgment instead of to the holy ones? [2]Do you not know that the holy ones will judge the

world? If the world is to be judged by you, are you unqualified for the lowest law courts? [3]Do you not know that we will judge angels? Then why not everyday matters? [4]If, therefore, you have courts for everyday matters, do you seat as judges people of no standing in the church? [5]I say this to shame you. Can it be that there is not one among you wise enough to be able to settle a case between brothers? [6]But rather brother goes to court against brother, and that before unbelievers?

[7]Now indeed [then] it is, in any case, a failure on your part that you have lawsuits against one another. Why not rather put up with injustice? Why not rather let yourselves be cheated? [8]Instead, you inflict injustice and cheat, and this to brothers. [9]Do you not know that the unjust will not inherit the kingdom of God? Do not be deceived; neither fornicators nor idolaters nor adulterers nor boy prostitutes nor sodomites [10]nor thieves nor the greedy nor drunkards nor slanderers nor robbers will inherit the kingdom of God. [11]That is what some of you used to be; but now you have had yourselves washed, you were sanctified, you were justified in the name of the Lord Jesus Christ and in the Spirit of our God.

If Paul could only see us today! Courts are, of course, places where justice is supposed to be done. But law schools rarely speak of justice. And in court the one with the best (and most expensive) lawyer usually wins. That is the problem, and that was the problem with courts at the time of Paul.

Paul appeals to Christian "wisdom" (6:5). This wisdom is a little different from, yet connected to the wisdom mentioned in the earlier homily on wisdom (cf. 2:6–16). Here Paul is referring to the wisdom traditions of Israel epitomized by the rulings of Solomon (cf. 2 Kgs 3). Some of these wisdom traditions spoke of a Spirit of Wisdom, a gift from God, that allowed one to see secular matters as God sees them (cf. Wis 7:22–30; Prv 8:1–36).

Paul refers to these Christian judges as "the holy ones" (6:2). It is clear from the parallel between "the holy ones" and "you," that he is referring to the Corinthians. The image of these "holy ones" judging the world is an image Paul also received from the late wisdom traditions of Israel. The Wisdom of Solomon described "the souls of the just" who "shall judge nations and rule over peoples" (Wis 3:1.8). Sirach writes: "Wisdom instructs her children and admonishes those who seek her. . . . He who obeys her judges nations" (Sir 4:11.15). Jesus in Matthew reflects this tradition as he promises his disciples: "Amen, I say to you that you who have followed me, in the new age, when the Son of Man is seated on his throne of glory, will yourselves sit on twelve thrones, judging the twelve tribes of Israel" (Mt 19:28).

To the extent Christians are "washed," "sanctified," and "justified," they should be able to fulfill this role. Their resources for wisdom lie in "the name of our Lord Jesus Christ and in the Spirit of our God" (6:11). Paul wrote in the homily on wisdom that this Spirit of God gives us a taste for the gifts of God, attunes us to the paradoxical ways of God. Here Paul takes a step further and asserts that this taste and attunement for things of God should give us the prudence to deal with human matters. For Paul then the act of civil justice is not so much based on the knowledge of all the details of the law, but on a firm attunement to God, a deep sense of God's ways, which then supposedly should give us a nudge about which course of action to take—functioning somewhat like our modern concept of conscience.

Thus Paul asks, "Why not rather let yourselves be cheated?" This thought is not going to sell business in a law practice. But it is the mind of Christ. It is this paradoxical, this apocalyptic reversal at the basis of Paul's theology: power looks like weakness.

For reflection. Christian attorneys in the Catholic tradition still have the custom of celebrating the "Red Mass" once a year, where they pray for the Holy Spirit to guide them in their profession. It is a celebration of the intense seriousness of the legal profession. It is also a challenge to see how civil justice in a Christian apocalyptic perspective is different than "lawyering" according to the deceits of this world.

53

"Why not rather let yourselves be cheated?" This is not a call to constant pacifism before criminal forces. There are times to fight back, times to defend oneself. But Paul here is challenging us with the insight that ultimately injustice is destroyed only by the crucifixion. There comes a time—and it can only come once—when each of us must die with Jesus. Jesus died a victim of injustice. To die in such a manner is a privilege. By weakness, God powerfully saves the world.

Sexual Immorality (6:12–20)

Turning to general sexual immorality (*porneia*), Paul starts with another favorite literary device of the Stoics, an imaginary conversation partner who objects to your positions. (Some of these objections are placed in quotes by the NAB.)

> [12]"Everything is lawful for me," but not everything is bene-ficial. "Everything is lawful for me," but I will not let myself be dominated by anything. [13]"Food for the stomach and the stomach for food," but God will do away with both the one and the other. The body, however, is not for immorality, but for the Lord, and the Lord is for the body; [14]God raised the Lord and will also raise us by his power.
>
> [14]Do you not know that your bodies are members of Christ? Shall I then take Christ's members and make them the members of a prostitute? Of course not! [16][Or] do you not know that anyone who joins himself to a prostitute becomes one body with her? For "the two," it says, "will become one flesh." [17]But whoever is joined to the Lord becomes one spirit with him. [18]Avoid immorality. Every other sin a person commits is outside the body, but the immoral person sins against his own body. [19]Do you not know that your body is a temple of the holy Spirit within you, whom you have from God, and that you are not your own? [20]For you have been purchased at a price. Therefore glorify God in your body.

Paul is probably thinking of the attitude that winked at the incest at Corinth (cf. 5:2) and describing it with the slogan, "Everything is lawful for me" (6:12; cf. 10:23). Interestingly, Paul does not immediately say, "No it isn't." Rather he says, "Yes, but." He apparently does not want to fall back on a legal discussion about what is legitimate and what is not. And as he will write later, "If you are guided by the Spirit, you are not under the Law" (Gal 5:18). Here he rather raises the question to the level of what is "beneficial" and what frees from being "dominated." In his explanation Paul shows he does not accept the libertine interpretation that maybe some Corinthians are following and which he himself may have been accused of.

The imaginary objector continues, "Food is for the stomach; the stomach, for food, but God will do away with both" (6:13). The argument seems to be that bodily functions are not that important. You just scratch your itches. When you get hungry you eat. When you get "aroused," you have sex. Sounds very modern.

Paul responds to both parts of the objector's argument. First, God will not do away with the body. "The body is . . . for the Lord, and the Lord is for the body" (6:13). God will raise our bodies just as he raised the body of Jesus (6:14). Thus the body is very important in God's apocalyptic plan. It is not just a part of this world which will be "done away with." It is capable of the transformation which takes place in the resurrection. Paul will explain this idea of resurrection more in chapter 15 of this letter.

Secondly, sex is not an ordinary bodily function like eating. Sex unites people. Having sex from a prostitute is not like buying a hot dog from a vendor. The sexual union brings you and the prostitute to a profound union, whether you like it or not. This union is very serious because we are already united even more profoundly with Christ. Our bodies are sacred. And what engages our body—the way sex does—is therefore sacred. In an earlier letter Paul wrote that the key to sexual morality was a sense of one's holiness (1 Thes 4:3–8).

Paul develops this part of the argument with three parallel statements, each beginning with "Do you not know?" (6:15, 16, 19). On the third round, Paul says it again by referring to the temple image he used earlier for the community (3:16). But here he is very clear how the temple image also applies to the individual person. "Your body is a temple of the Holy Spirit." Just as our body gives us a sense of spacial location, of "insides" and "outsides," connecting the Holy Spirit with our body allows Paul to speak of the Spirit "within you." Later Paul will speak of the Holy Spirit "who dwells in you" (Rom 8:9, 11; cf. Gal 4:6).

For Paul the precious character of the body is also manifest by the redemptive death of Jesus. The connection between Jesus' role and the body is not as clear as the connection between the Holy Spirit and the body. But Paul brings in Jesus' death as an illustration of how we are not our own, to do with ourselves as we wish. We belong to Jesus. We have been purchased at a great price. We must thus glorify God in our body!

This portrayal of Jesus' death is another attempt to interpret the death as a saving or good thing. We saw above how Paul assimilated this death to the paschal sacrifice (5:7). Here Paul turns to the market place (maybe the slave market) for images by which he can interpret this horrible death. The image is that of a purchase. "You have been purchased at a price" (6:20; cf. 7:23). This imagery is behind the complex and widespread attempts in the New Testament to deal with Jesus' death as "redemption" (*lytrosis*) or a "ransom" (*lytron*). This imagery has led to a great deal of wasted theology when the image was pushed too far. This imagery does not intend to identify anyone *to whom* the price or ransom was paid—neither the devil nor God. The price was not payed to anybody! It was just paid! The imagery intends to say one thing: our salvation is at a great price! This idea then leads to the sense of belonging to Christ.

For reflection. Part of the difficulty of living a Christian life in our culture lies in the distorted picture of sex which pervades it. Sex is seen as a commodity. Even if our culture does not condone prostitution, it sells sex through its commercials. It sells sex in the vast bulk of our entertainment. The result is the distinct impression that sex is like your new car. You want to keep it shiny and looking good to impress others. You do a little test driving before you settle on one model. And you can trade it in when it looks a bit dumpy. We may be reacting to a time when sex was considered basically evil. But we seem to have moved from one extreme to the other. Paul has not given us here a complete view of sexual morality, but as usual he points out the theological foundation of that morality.

IV

Questions about Marriage and Celibacy
(7:1–40)

One of the delegations from Corinth must have brought over a series of questions about marriage and different forms of celibacy. Paul acknowledges a distinct question when he begins a part of his letter with the words, "Now in regard to . . ." (7:1, 25; 8:1; 12:1; 16:1). In chapter 7 of our letter, Paul picks up the first question, marriage and celibacy. Actually, we can distinguish at least seven different topics related to marriage and states of life. Perhaps the Corinthians had seven distinct questions; perhaps Paul is explaining more than they want to know.

We are used to church leaders giving much direction for marriage, yet Paul is writing long before Christian marriage was considered sacramental, when marriage was far more a contractual matter regulated by the state, much like the state regulated the sale of property. We need to seek in the text why Paul is offering such pointed advice on marriage.

Sex in Marriage (7:1–7)

Paul starts his instructions with the words of an imaginary conversation partner, probably voicing an attitude of some Corinthians.

> [1]Now in regard to the matters about which you wrote: "It is a good thing for a man not to touch a woman," [2]but because of cases of immorality every man should have his own wife, and every woman her own husband. [3]The husband should fulfill his duty toward his wife, and likewise the wife toward her husband. [4]A wife does not have authority over her own

body, but rather her husband, and similarly a husband does not have authority over his own body, but rather his wife. [5]Do not deprive each other, except perhaps by mutual consent for a time, to be free for prayer, but then return to one another, so that Satan may not tempt you through your lack of self-control. [6]This I say by way of concession, however, not as a command. [7]Indeed, I wish everyone to be as I am, but each has a particular gift from God, one of one kind and one of another.

If "everything is lawful for me" (6:12) represents one group in Corinth, then "good not to touch a woman" must represent a very different group. This group seems to advocate a type of rigorism, pushing sexual abstinence even for married people. We know of several Hellenistic philosophical and religious groups that saw everything bodily or sexual as bad. Paul has just explained that such a view is not correct (cf. 6:12–20).

Addressing this question Paul admits some value of sexual abstinence, "to be free for prayer" (7:5). Such a view seems to relate to an ancient although rare tradition in the Old Testament which connected sexual abstinence with approaching God (cf. Ex 19:15; cf. 1 Sm 21:5; Tb 8:4 Vulgate).

What Paul stresses here is mutual consent. No spouse can make the decision for the other. The way Paul gives a direction for a wife and then repeats it for the husband aligns Paul with a Roman view of marriage which stressed balanced mutual consent. The Jewish view tended to give all the power to the husband.

Paul apparently was celibate at this time, either never married or a widow (cf. 7:8). He clearly recommends this life. He is careful, however, to avoid any commands. This matter is one of recognizing the divine gift each person has received.

For reflection. Paul's initial stress on "duty" and "authority" looks awkward to many today reading these instructions about marital love. It is a puzzle why Paul took such a legalistic approach. However, his legal approach was definitely from Roman law, where husband and wives both had rights and duties. We see therefore Paul's efforts to stress mutual relations. He repeats instructions for both husbands and for wives. He stresses the importance of mutual consent. Mutual consent requires looking at the matter through your partner's eyes. In marital relations, two people—while remaining two—become one. Is this mutuality something I need to develop in my marriage?

Advice to the Unmarried and the Married (7:8–11)

Remaining as in one's present state is Paul's advice to the unmarried and his command to the married:

> [8]Now to the unmarried and to widows I say: it is good for them to remain as they are, as I do, [9]but if they cannot exercise self-control they should marry, for it is better to marry than to be on fire. [10]To the married, however, I give this instruction (not I, but the Lord): a wife should not separate from her husband—[11]and if she does separate she must either remain single or become reconciled to her husband—and a husband should not divorce his wife.

Again Paul declares celibacy as "a good thing" without giving a lot of explanation, except for a personal testimony from his own life. The portrayal of marriage as a remedy for lust ("fire") here and in the preceding instruction ("Satan") is not very positive. If we saw the sexual indulgence he saw in Greece, we might be saying the same thing. Corinth was one of the centers of the cult of Aphrodite, the goddess of sexual love. On the Acrocorinth behind the city, reportedly a thousand sacred prostitutes working day and night helped men in their "religious devotion" to this goddess.

The "instruction" to the married is basically what we read in the gospels. Paul is very clear. This is an instruction from the Lord. No divorce. Again following the style of Roman law, Paul like Mark (cf. Mk 10:11–12) repeats the injunction for both men and women. Matthew, however, following the style of Jewish law, speaks only about men (Mt 5:31–32; 19:1–9).

Mixed Marriages (7:12–16)

After his description of Jesus' view on divorce, Paul continues the topic as it regards marriages where only one of the couple is Christian.

> [12]To the rest I say (not the Lord): if any brother has a wife who is an unbeliever, and she is willing to go on living with him, he should not divorce her; [13]and if any woman has a husband who is an unbeliever, and he is willing to go on living with her, she should not divorce her husband. [14]For the unbelieving husband is made holy through his wife, and the unbelieving wife is made holy through the brother. Otherwise your children would be unclean, whereas in fact they are holy.
> [15]If the unbeliever separates, however, let him separate. The brother or sister is not bound in such cases; God has called you to peace. [16]For how do you know, wife, whether you will save your husband; or how do you know, husband, whether you will save your wife?

Paul starts by saying that divorce is not necessary in a mixed marriage. That statement might sound surprising to us. However, Paul was familiar with a tradition that denounced mixed marriages, even to the extent of urging one to divorce the non-believing spouse along with the children born from that marriage (cf. Ezra 9:1–10:44). Paul's statement here would make sense if a group in Corinth were in fact advocating such a view. Although Paul recognizes the intense unity and intimacy marriage brings the spouses especially in matters of religion, he sees no reason for breaking up households simply because one of the spouses is an "outsider" in the faith. This is an important observation for understanding Paul's views about "insiders" and "outsiders" in the church.

Although at the time of Paul households tended to conform in their religion, especially in the religion of the head of the household (cf. Acts 10:2; 16:15, 33), the situation Paul is addressing in Corinth now shows that families were sometimes split by an individual making his or her own choice about becoming a Christian. Such a division in a household could have been heart-wrenching and the source of enormous strife (cf. Mt 10:34–36). Christianity may have been unusual in this recognition of individual choice. It may also have been viewed as destructive of "family values."

When Paul describes the value of believer and non-believer remaining married, he speaks of a type of holiness passing from one person to another, from believing spouse to non-believing spouse and then to the children. The idea is close to the "contagious" character of clean and unclean found in the Old Testament (cf. Lv 12–15). In fact Paul's seemingly inadvertent contrast between "unclean" and "holy" (7:14) suggests this Old Testament view is in the back of his head. That holiness could be "communicable" without a personal decision seems strange to us, who place such an enormous stress on personal decision and responsibility. Paul is suggesting that a whole family —believers and non-believers—could be holy because one member is holy, because one member in some way represents the whole family.

Paul then addresses the situation of strife brought on by one spouse becoming a Christian. His recommendation is divorce. The value of peace is more important than that of the permanence of the marriage.

This recommendation seems astounding in the light of what Paul has just said about no divorce—based on Jesus' own teaching (7:10–11). The Catholic legal tradition has carefully defined this exception, contrasting it from a consummated sacramental marriage—the Pauline privilege. As a matter of fact, Jesus' instructions regarded all marriages. Neither Jesus nor Paul were making any distinction between sacramental or non-sacramental marriages. Jesus said, "No way!" Paul says,

"There's a way!" As a matter of fact, Matthew in his reporting of Jesus' instruction also introduced an exception to the blanket rule, "except for immorality" (Mt 5:32;19:9).

What we see here is the way the first Christians understood the teachings of Jesus. They understood these teachings as those of a prophet not those of legislator. Prophets drove home a point even by exaggerating things. When Jesus told us to pluck out our eye or cut off our hand to avoid sin (Mk 9:43–48), he was not commanding us to mutilate ourselves. He was exaggerating. By this prophetic hyperbole Jesus was driving home the point that sin is much worse than any physical disability. Paul and Matthew apparently understood the teachings of Jesus about marriage as driving home the value of indissoluble unity without providing the legal technicalities of what this means in every case.

For reflection. What an awesome picture Paul draws here of Christian family life. One spouse is made holy by the other—even if the first spouse is "unbelieving." The children are made holy by the faith of the parents—even if they are too young to make any decision. God in effect blesses the family through the faith of perhaps just one believing spouse. In this intense solidarity of holiness, there is no need for each individual to conform to the faith of the other. Such unfortunate clashes of faith can still fit into God's effective love for the whole family.

Staying in One's Social State (7:17–24)

Paul digresses for a moment to consider two other social conditions, in both cases denying any great importance to the condition and recommending staying where one was called:

> [17]Only, everyone should live as the Lord has assigned, just as God called each one. I give this order in all the churches. [18]Was someone called after he had been circumcised? He

should not try to undo his circumcision. Was an uncircumcised person called? He should not be circumcised. [19]Circumcision means nothing, and uncircumcision means nothing; what matters is keeping God's commandments. [20]Everyone should remain in the state in which he was called.

[21]Were you a slave when you were called? Do not be concerned but, even if you gain your freedom, make the most of it. [22]For the slave called in the Lord is a freed person in the Lord, just as the free person who has been called is a slave of Christ. [23]You have been purchased at a great price. Do not become slaves to human beings. [24]Brothers, everyone should continue before God in the state in which he was called.

In this instruction about foreskins and slavery, we see a vignette of the Corinthian church. It must have been composed of very diverse people. We know of no other private association or club at the time of Paul that tried to mix such a diverse group of people as Paul's churches. A Dionysus club did exist in which senators and slaves were both members, but in it the senators acted like senators, and the slaves, slaves. Paul tried to compress diverse people into a group where the distinction between Jew or Gentile, free or slave, rich or poor—later he will add male or female (Gal 3:28)—did not count for much.

Paul is not really against shifting one's social status. In fact he gives a piece of advice to the slave who becomes free, "Make the most of it" (7:21). His repeated admonition to remain in one's social state appears above all as an instruction to understand one's status by a relation to God, not to other people. As the prophets long ago stated, keeping God's commandments is more important than any ritual sign. Recognizing our redemption and subsequent relationship to Christ is more important than any social condition.

Staying in One's Marital State (7:25–35)

With this perspective Paul returns to the issue of marriage and celibacy.

^{25}Now in regard to virgins I have no commandment from the Lord, but I give my opinion as one who by the Lord's mercy is trustworthy. ^{26}So this is what I think best because of the present distress; that it is a good thing for a person to remain as he is. ^{27}Are you bound to a wife? Do not seek a separation. Are you free of a wife? Then do not look for a wife. ^{28}If you marry, however, you do not sin, nor does an unmarried woman sin if she marries; but such people will experience affliction in their earthly life, and I would like to spare you that.

^{29}I tell you, brothers, the time is running out. From now on, let those having wives act as not having them, ^{30}those weeping as not weeping, those rejoicing as not rejoicing, those buying as not owning, ^{31}those using the world as not using it fully. For the world in its present form is passing away.

^{32}I should like you to be free of anxieties. An unmarried man is anxious about the things of the Lord, how he may please the Lord. ^{33}But a married man is anxious about the things of the world, how he may please his wife, ^{34}and he is divided. An unmarried woman or a virgin is anxious about the things of the Lord, so that she may be holy in both body and spirit. A married woman, on the other hand, is anxious about the things of the world, how she may please her husband. ^{35}I am telling you this for your own benefit, not to impose a restraint upon you, but for the sake of propriety and adherence to the Lord without distraction.

A third time in this chapter Paul urges people to remain as they are. This time he gives an explicit motivation, "because of the present distress" (7:26). A line or two later he seems to say the same thing, "I tell you, brothers, the time is running out" (7:29). Our world and our worldly lives are in an advanced stage of terminal illness. Now is not the time to be thinking of a career change.

All through this instruction, Paul gives the edge to celibacy, the state of the unmarried. The married experience "affliction in their earthly life" (7:28). The anxieties of the married person are "about the things of the world" (7:33), including one's spouse. Married people know that this is true. Marriage and especially family roots one in this world. Sound investments, a stable job, health insurance, even social status become very important. Your children's lives are deeply affected by all of these things—even if you want to remain aloof. There is no sin in this, just affliction.

However, when Paul gives the reason for all this advice, he states, "I should like you to be free of anxieties" But then he immediately says, "An unmarried man is anxious about the things of the Lord, how he may please the Lord" (7:32). Although his focus is on the anxieties of the married, something suggests that Paul recognizes how unhealthy anxieties can affect also the dedicated celibate. If Paul really wants people to be free of anxieties, then he does not seem to be approving of the man or woman "anxious about the things of the Lord." Paul drops this subject and later stresses "adherence to the Lord without distraction" (7:35). But perhaps he is advocating—for both the married and the celibate—a type of joyful and peaceful adherence which roots one in the grace of the world to come.

It is spiritual freedom that Paul is advocating here, the freedom of the eschatological world. The poetic description of radical detachment, at the center of this section (7:29–31) is a call to spiritual freedom. At the time of Paul a group of philosophers, called Cynics, tried to practice this radical detachment. Paul probably admired something of their attitude. But Paul describes the Christian motivation of this detachment, the nearness of the Kingdom of God. Soon the Christian martyrs would practice in dramatic detail the forms of detachment that Paul describes here. Before the great persecutions arrived, Paul saw in social detachment and especially in dedicated celibacy the same world denying attitude of the martyr.

For reflection. Am I anxious? Why? Should I be anxious?

Domestic Virgins and Widows (7:36–40)

Before concluding this general topic Paul gives his advice on two other topics:

> [36]If anyone thinks he is behaving improperly toward his virgin, and if a critical moment has come and so it has to be, let him do as he wishes. He is committing no sin; let them get married. [37]The one who stands firm in his resolve, however, who is not under compulsion but has power over his own will, and has made up his mind to keep his virgin, will be doing well. [38]So then the one who marries his virgin does well; the one who does not marry her will do better.
>
> [39]A wife is bound to her husband as long as he lives. But if her husband dies, she is free to be married to whomever she wishes, provided that it be in the Lord. [40]She is more blessed, though, in my opinion, if she remains as she is, and I think that I too have the Spirit of God.

In Greek the first paragraph is more ambiguous than the NAB. Paul may be speaking of a father who must decide whether to give his daughter in marriage or let her remain a virgin. Paul may also be speaking of fiancés thinking of a life without sex, a sort of spiritual marriage. The only thing we see clearly here is Paul's insistence that the matter be decided in great freedom, without any pressure.

Regarding the widow, Paul asserts her freedom to marry again. We do not know what Paul meant by a marriage "in the Lord." There were no church weddings in those days, no sense of marriage as a sacrament. But as Paul has said before, the eschatological stance of the unmarried and the virgin is a better choice.

All through this chapter Paul has been reflecting on the weight he wants to give his statements. Sometimes he weights it with the authority of Christ (7:10), most of the time he calls his statement "an opinion" (7:25, 40) or a "concession" as opposed to a "command" (7:6). Why is Paul so delicate here, whereas in other places he resembles a bulldozer? He really thinks his opinions are important, "as one who is trustworthy" (7:25) or as one who has "the Spirit of God" (7:40). But through this chapter Paul has insisted on the gifts each person receives from God and how one's social status and especially one's marital status is rooted in a gift from God. Paul knows better than to force God's love of each individual into a mold, into some rule that applies to all. In this area the mysterious wisdom of God is very much mystery.

For reflection. Without knowing it, Paul in this chapter started a tradition in the Christian church of intense concern about the marriages of its members. Actually the tradition took off centuries later when the bishops of the Western Empire needed to step into the void caused by the collapse of the civil government. However, the energy Paul expends in this chapter drove home the message that marriage is not just another civil contract. Marriage demands the intense mutual respect characteristic of Christian love. Jesus wanted marriage to return to the ideals of the beginnings. Holiness is somehow passed through a family. And in an apocalyptic world, one's marital and social status was also a statement about the nearness of God's kingdom.

In the same way Paul here appears to stand at the head also of a long tradition of religious celibacy. During the persecutions Christians needed no special ways of living the life of the Kingdom of God. Martyrdom was all too close. A few centuries later when the persecutions of the West ceased, religious virtuosos sought a special way of rooting their lives outside of this passing world. The desert fathers and mothers arose on the scene, rejecting marriage along with other structures of social status.

From Paul we see marriage and celibacy as divine gifts fitting into God's mysterious plan, and fitting into God's church. Reflecting again on the gifts in the church, Paul will later state that all gifts are for "building up the church" (14:12). The desert fathers and mothers will show how celibacy witnesses in and to the church the presence of the end times. A later biblical writer will in the name of Paul describe marriage as a symbol of the love between Christ and his church (Eph 5:22–33).

What gift of social or marital status have I received? How can my gift build up Christ's church?

V

Warnings Against Idolatry and Other Matters

(8:1—11:1)

Chapter 8 begins a response to another question ("Now, in regard to . . ."). The topic is "meat sacrificed to idols." After treating this topic somewhat, Paul in chapter 9 digresses to his rights as an apostle. He defends his ministry and describes his efforts to adapt to all groups. Chapter 10 then begins with a type of biblical homily warning against idolatry and immorality (10:1–13). This leads Paul to reflect on the Lord's Supper (10:14–22) and finally to return to the topic of meat sacrificed to idols (10:15–11:1).

We could probably break up this section in many ways, but the repetition of topics at the beginning of chapter 8 and the end of chapter 10 suggests a framework designating a unit, what scholars call an "inclusion." This sort of rambling, appropriate in a letter, means we can break up the section for examination in any practical way. We can only guess at what led Paul to move from one topic to the other. Once in a while we note a thematic thread of continuity.

Meat Sacrificed to Idols (8:1–13)

Introducing the first topic, Paul picks up an objection to any restricting rules. He then answers the objection. The development includes two additional objections and Paul's responses.

[1]Now in regard to meat sacrificed to idols: we realize that "all of us have knowledge"; knowledge inflates with pride, but

love builds up. ²If anyone supposes he knows something, he does not yet know as he ought to know. ³But if one loves God, one is known by him.

⁴So about the eating of meat sacrificed to idols: we know that "there is no idol in the world," and that "there is no God but one." ⁵Indeed, even though there are so-called gods in heaven and on earth (there are, to be sure, many "gods" and many "lords"), ⁶yet for us there is

one God, the Father,

from whom all things are and for whom we exist,

and one Lord, Jesus Christ,

through whom all things are and through whom we exist.

⁷But not all have this knowledge. There are some who have been so used to idolatry up until now that, when they eat meat sacrificed to idols, their conscience, which is weak, is defiled.

⁸"Now food will not bring us closer to God. We are no worse off if we do not eat, nor are we better off if we do." ⁹[Quotations not in NAB.] But make sure that this liberty of yours in no way becomes a stumbling block to the weak. ¹⁰If someone sees you, with your knowledge, reclining at table in the temple of an idol, may not his conscience too, weak as it is, be "built up" to eat the meat sacrificed to idols? ¹¹Thus through your knowledge, the weak person is brought to destruction, the brother for whom Christ died. ¹²When you sin in this way against your brothers and wound their consciences, weak as they are, you are sinning against Christ. ¹³Therefore, if food causes my brother to sin, I will never eat meat again, so that I may not cause by brother to sin.

The imaginary conversation partner begins, "All of us have knowledge" (8:1). The argument will be an appeal to an enlightened understanding of idolatry. As this partner would explain, "There is no idol in the world" (8:4).

This enlightened approach to idols stems back some five hundred years, when the exilic and post-exilic prophets ridiculed idolatry:

> An idol, cast by a craftsman, which the smith plates with gold and fits with silver chains? Mulberry wood, the choice portion which a skilled craftsman picks out for himself. Choosing timber that will not rot, to set up an idol that will not be unsteady. . . . He says the soldering is good, and he fastens it with nails to steady it (Is 40:19–20; 41:7).

About one hundred years before Paul and the Corinthian church, a Jewish sage wrote:

> Who termed gods things made by human hands:
> Gold and silver, the product of art, and likenesses
>   of beasts, or useless stone, the work of an ancient
>   hand.
> A carpenter may saw out a suitable tree and skillfully
>   scrape off all its bark . . .
> This wood he models with listless skill, and patterns it
>   on the image of a man or makes it resemble some
>   worthless beast. (Wis 13:10–14)

In effect, then the enlightened Corinthian has learned the lesson well. Idols are nothing, and for those "in the know," this is all a big joke.

Christian faith for Paul, however, is more than knowledge, more than an ideology. It is a call to love. So Paul answers by contrasting "knowledge" with "love." In this contrast he comes up with one of the "flip to the passive" sayings which he likes. "Knowing" can lead to a deficient form of knowledge, but love leads to use *being known* by God (8:2). By this saying Paul wants to insist not only on the superiority of love over knowledge but also on the initiative and activity of God in our lives. What we do is a lot less important than what God does for us.

Paul does acknowledge the position of the enlightened Corinthian. Even though people talk about many gods, there really is only one God. He can even strengthen this position by adding what appears to be an early Christian credal statement, one of the earliest statements of doctrine in the profession of which one Christian could recognize another. The creed speaks of God, the Father, as the unique source and purpose of all creation and Christ, the Lord, as the unique medium through whom all things exist.

We note the very careful attribution of functions to God and to Christ. God, the Father, is the creator. Paul never places Christ in that function. Here also Paul insists on God as the goal or purpose of creation. This is a very Jewish view. God is both the beginning and the end, not only the creator but also the judge. All things have their meaning and purpose in the light of God. If Paul wrote Colossians at the end of his career, he shifted. There Paul will write that all things are not only "through" Christ," but also "for him" (Col 1:16).

The creed found in our text carefully describes Jesus as the medium "through whom" God creates. Such a faith would affirm a basic christic mark on all that is created. Just as the artist's medium determines the end result and can be identified by examining the end result, so Christ, as the medium of creation, has left a determining element on all that is real and should be recognized by those who truly see reality—at least with the believer's eyes. Likewise such a faith would seem to hold that Jesus existed at the time of creation, and therefore preexisted his human life. When Old Testament sages wrote of God's wisdom, personifying it as a person alongside of God, they said many of the same things (cf. Prv 8:1–36; Wis 7:22–30; Sir 24:1–31).

After continuing to dance with the imaginary conversation partner for a while (8:8), Paul returns to the main point he wants to make about meat offered to the idols. Granted the enlightened Christian is strong and not really affected by what-ever ceremony the meats were part of, Paul knows of other

Christians who are "weak" (8:7, 9). They are not enlightened and may interpret another's consumption of meat as an apostasy to the idols.

Almost for sure these "weak" are also the economically poor in Corinth. These are people who almost never ate meat. Their diet was a monotonous gruel. For the poor meat was available only at the public religious feasts, where meat was passed out free. Thus in their minds meat and pagan religion were linked.

The "strong" would be the rich for whom hearty and meaty meals were common. Should they care about the foolish ideas of the weak? Paul answers the question by saying something very close to Matthew 25:31–46, the parable of the sheep and goats at the last judgment where Jesus clearly identifies himself with the poor and the needy. Wounding the consciences of the weak is in fact "sinning against Christ" (8:12).

According to Luke, writing the Acts of the Apostles, the issue of meat offered to idols was discussed and decided in a council in Jerusalem some six years earlier, around A.D. 49. Acts describes Paul as present at that meeting contributing to the final determination, that gentile Christians among other things were to abstain totally from meat offered to idols (Acts 15:29). Paul's own treatment of the topic and his total silence about the council of A.D. 49 argue strongly that Luke did not get his information from Paul and had only a vague knowledge about the Jewish Christian decision, which may in fact have been in force for Christians only around Jerusalem.

For reflection. The early church struggled with issues, especially how it was to live and be faithful in the midst of a basically hostile culture. Where should we draw the line? To some Paul appeared to be capitulating to conservative stupidity. To the Jerusalem church at the time, he was probably a wild-eyed liberal. Interesting how the church continues to struggle.

Paul seems to say that Christians have the right to eat meat, even that which was part of a pagan religious ceremony. However, he senses the necessity to give up this right for the sake of a brother or sister in Christ. Could this approach be a method of resolving conflicts in the church today?

Is there any analogue today to "meat offered to idols"? It would be an element of our culture that really looks repugnant to Christian faith. Yet it would be something we could rationalize or justify because first, in itself it is just stupid and secondly, it is very difficult to avoid. It would be something evaluated in different ways by "the weak" and "the strong" in our church today.

Paul's Rights as an Apostle (9:1–27)

At this point in the letter, something led Paul to think about his own authority and rigorously defend it, especially as regards his *non-use* of his right to be paid as an apostle.

[1]Am I not free? Am I not an apostle? Have I not seen Jesus our Lord? Are you not my work in the Lord? [2]Although I may not be an apostle for others, certainly I am for you, for you are the seal of my apostleship in the Lord.

[3]My defense against those who would pass judgment on me is this. [4]Do we not have the right to eat and drink? [5]Do we not have the right to take along a Christian wife, as do the rest of the apostles, and the brothers of the Lord, and Kephas? [6]Or is it only myself and Barnabas who do not have the right not to work? [7]Who ever serves as a soldier at his own expense? Who plants a vineyard without eating its produce? Or who shepherds a flock without using some of the milk from the flock? [8]Am I saying this on human authority, or does not the law also speak of these things? [9]It is written in the law of Moses, "You shall not muzzle an ox while it is treading out the grain." Is God concerned about oxen, [10]or is he not really speaking for our sake? It was written for our sake, because the plowman should plow in hope, and the thresher in hope of receiving a share. [11]If we have sown spiritual seed for you, is it a great thing that we reap a material harvest from you? [12]If others share this rightful claim on you, do not we still more?

Yet we have not used this right. On the contrary, we endure everything so as not to place an obstacle to the gospel of Christ. ¹³Do you not know that those who perform the temple services eat (what) belongs to the temple, and those who minister at the altar share in the sacrificial offerings? ¹⁴In the same way, the Lord ordered that those who preach the gospel should live by the gospel.

¹⁵I have not used any of these rights, however, nor do I write this that it be done so in my case, I would rather die. Certainly no one is going to nullify my boast. ¹⁶If I preach the gospel, this is no reason for me to boast, for an obligation has been imposed on me, and woe to me if I do not preach it! ¹⁷If I do so willingly, I have a recompense, but if unwillingly, then I have been entrusted with a stewardship. ¹⁸What then is my recompense? That, when I preach, I offer the gospel free of charge so as not to make full use of my right in the gospel.

¹⁹Although I am free in regard to all, I have made myself a slave to all so as to win over as many as possible. ²⁰To the Jews I became like a Jew to win over Jews; to those under the law I became like one under the law—though I myself am not under the law—to win over those under the law. ²¹To those outside the law I became like one outside the law—though I am not outside God's law but within the law of Christ—to win over those outside the law. ²²To the weak I became weak, to win over the weak. I have become all things to all, to save at least some. ²³All this I do for the sake of the gospel, so that I too may have a share in it.

²⁴Do you not know that the runners in the stadium all run in the race, but only one wins the prize? Run so as to win. ²⁵Every athlete exercises discipline in every way. They do it to win a perishable crown, but we an imperishable one. ²⁶Thus I do not run aimlessly; I do not fight as if I were shadowboxing. ²⁷No, I drive my body and train it, for fear that, after having preached to others, I myself should be disqualified.

When Paul in the preceding section described his willingness to give up any right to eat meat for the sake of his weak brothers, something must have clicked in his mind about another matter of giving up rights. This transition also seems to have pushed Paul's button, because a tone of anger suddenly rises. Paul speaks about needing to defend himself "against those who would pass judgment" on him as an apostle (9:3).

What was this "judgment" or attack all about? It seems someone in Corinth questioned whether Paul was really an apostle. The question is a good one. According to Luke, Paul would not have qualified. Luke really thought the world of Paul, but for Luke to be an apostle required at least three things: to have accompanied Jesus from the time of Jesus' baptism, to witness Jesus' resurrection, and to receive some sort of commission. We see these job specifications in the discussion about who might replace Judas (Acts 1:21–26). On the first point Paul would have missed the boat.

Paul, on the other hand, insists that he is an apostle. At the beginning of this section Paul makes four rhetorical questions which in effect are four statements, best read as synonymous parallels. He is free. He is an apostle. He has seen the Lord. The Corinthians are his work in the Lord (9:1–2). The first two describe his status or office. The second two describe the basis of that status or office. To be an apostle in "freedom" means to have witnessed the risen Christ and to have created a Christian community. Paul's paschal witness is a bit out of sync with that of the Twelve, something he will discuss again later in this letter (cf. 15:5–9), but it is of the same order. And Paul has sealed this office by his work founding vibrant communities. Paul might appear as a "johnny-come-lately," but in the eyes of faith he is on the same level as the Twelve.

Since in the rest of this section, Paul focuses a great deal on his offering the gospel free of charge, this refusal to accept payment must have been part of any attack on his apostolic authority. Why such a refusal could be a problem requires understanding the system of patronage at Corinth and in this Greco-Roman world. This social world formed a very steep pyramid, a few very rich at the top, a huge foundation of very poor and a narrow band of middle class. The rich both expressed their civic duties and flaunted their wealth by various forms of patronage. Among other things they provided buildings for clubs and associations to use. They supported public works. In turn they were lavished with honors, either publically or within the associations they supported as patrons.

As it would appear, the early church met its logistic needs by using this system of patronage. In the next generation, we see bishop-elders offering hospitality to itinerant preachers and in return receiving power and honor in their noble office (cf. 1 Tm 3:1–2; 5:17–23). Paul seems here to have flatly refused any patronage from the Corinthians. One tradition describes Paul earning his livelihood as a tentmaker (Acts 18:3). This refusal could well have been received like a slap in the face.

So Paul starts by insisting that he not only could have received this patronage, he could have demanded it (9:4–14). Somehow the issue of his celibate status got involved here as part of the criticism (9:5), but the stress remains on the issue of remuneration for his preaching. The lack of any such remuneration for Paul therefore does *not* mean that he had no right to it, but rather that he willingly and boldly renounced that right (9:12, 15).

Paul spends then the rest of the section explaining why this renouncement should not have been taken as a slap in the face. He first of all speaks of a compelling obligation he experiences to preach the gospel. Willing or unwilling, as a voluntary paid worker or as involuntary but high class slave (*oikonomos*), he must preach this gospel of Christ (9:16–17). The only real recompense he experiences is simply in the fact that he is presenting this gospel to others—seen precisely because he is not doing it for money (9:18).

As mentioned earlier Paul's status or office is both being an apostle and being free. He never explains what he means by that freedom—unless it lies in his rights and his right to renounce these rights. But here Paul describes the paradoxical character of that freedom. In this freedom he makes himself a slave (9:19). In this freedom from the Law, he makes himself subject to the Law, like the Jews (9:20). In his subjection to the Law of Christ, he lives as a Gentile not subject to the Law (9:21). In his strength, Paul makes himself weak. We are not sure exactly what Paul concretely meant by these descriptions, but the main point is clear. Paul's focus is on the people to whom he is ministering. He is willing to become like those to whom he ministers, Jews, Gentiles, the weak, in order to minister more effectively. He becomes "all things to all."

This is not an easy life. It can be downright painful. But the pain here is like the pain of an athlete. ("No pain, no gain.") There is some sense to it. As they train, athletes groan and grunt, but they do not slump in depression. All the more, Paul explains, the painful life of an apostle can involve deep satisfaction and intense determination.

For reflection. There are several chapters in the letters of Paul that Christian ministers should meditate on, and 1 Corinthians 9 is one them. The last part especially challenges any leader in the church. Paul describes his "pantomorphous" ministry. He adapts to whomever he works with. There is no set image for himself which he uses to start the ministerial relationship. We could imagine Paul looking like a "bum" on skid row, or like a polished gentleman among the rich. Before Paul Jesus irritated the ministry establishment by eating with sinners. He did not look like a good minister.

Maybe it was easier to do that in the first generation of Christians, before the ministry got "established." This first generation were all trailblazers of one sort or another. Yet, Paul here seems to have run against several social stereotypes thrown against him. And one reason for using scripture is to remind us always of how it was. Scripture allows us all to be "first generation Christians."

Warning against Overconfidence (10:1–13)

Paul drops the reflections on himself and moves back toward the issue of idolatry. The thoughts he offers now consist of reflections on stories from Exodus and Numbers about the Israelites in the Sinai desert. The thoughts here are only loosely related to the central topic of this section, meat offered to idols, yet they appear to be carefully worked out. Hence, Paul probably is drawing again from his file cabinet of homilies. Seeing this section as part of a pre-composed unit would explain its literary form as well as its severe tone in the present context of eating food, which Paul earlier acknowledged as making us "no worse off" and "no better off" (8:8).

[1]I do not want you to be unaware, brothers, that our ancestors were all under the cloud and all passed through the sea, [2]and all of them were baptized into Moses in the cloud and in the sea. [3]All ate the same spiritual food, [4]and all drank the same spiritual drink, for they drank from a spiritual rock that followed them, and the rock was the Christ. [5]Yet God was not pleased with most of them, for they were struck down in the desert.

[6]These things happened as examples for us, so that we might not desire evil things, as they did. [7]And do not become idolaters, as some of them did, as it is written, "The people sat down to eat and drink, and rose up to revel." [8]Let us not indulge in immorality as some of them did, and twenty-three thousand fell within a single day. [9]Let us not test Christ as some of them did, and suffered death by serpents. [10]Do not grumble as some of them did, and suffered death by the destroyer. [11]These things happened to them as an example, and they have been written down as a warning to us, on whom the end of the ages has come. [12]Therefore, whoever thinks he is standing secure should take care not to fall. [13]No trial has come to you but what is human. God is faithful and will not let you be tried beyond your strength; but with the trial he will also provide a way out, so that you may be able to bear it.

Paul begins this section by calling up images from Exodus 13–17. In the Old Testament we read:

The Lord preceded them, in the daytime by means of a column of cloud to show them the way, and at night by means of a column of fire to give them light. Thus they could travel both day and night. Neither the column of cloud by day nor the column of fire by night ever left its place in front of the people. (Ex 13:21–22)

The Israelites marched into the midst of the sea on dry land, with the water like a wall to their right and to their left. (Ex 14:22)

Nothing is mentioned in these texts about baptism, but Paul associates both images of the cloud and the sea with baptism, perhaps because both images refer to the beginning or initiating experience of Israel. Paul uses an expression we cannot find anywhere else, being "baptized into Moses." In later writings Paul speaks of being baptized into Christ (Gal 3:27; Rom 6:3), which refers to the Christian's participation in the death and resurrection of Jesus. It is very difficult to figure out what Paul could have meant by being baptized "into Moses."

In the Old Testament we read likewise about the special food and drink of the Israelites:

Then the Lord said to Moses, "I will now rain down bread from heaven for you. Each day the people are to go out and gather their daily bread; thus will I test them, to see whether they follow my instructions or not. . . ." The Israelites ate this manna for forty years, until they came to settled land; they ate manna until they reached the borders of Canaan. (Ex 16:4, 35)

The Lord answered Moses, "Go over there in front of the people, along with some of the elders of Israel, holding in your hand, as you go, the staff with which you struck the river. I will be standing there in front of you on the rock in Horeb. Strike the rock, and the water will flow from it for the people to drink." This Moses did, in the presence of the elders of Israel. (Ex 17:5–6)

Nothing in the texts speaks about the rock moving or following the Israelites. Jewish readers of this text, however, must have wondered how the Israelites continued to drink once they moved from this rock. Actually in at least one Jewish re-writing of this story, more or less contemporary with the New Testament, the rock in this story moves (cf. Pseudo-Philo 10:3). Paul thus appears to be drawing, not directly on the Old Testament text, but on the interpreted reading of these biblical texts, which can be found in the contemporary Jewish legends. Just as later Jewish storytellers felt free to change details in the biblical stories, so Paul here adds the identification of the rock with Christ.

Such an addition might be just a quaint allegorical reading or it might be something much deeper. Earlier Paul in this letter wrote of a mysterious wisdom hidden in the past now revealed through the Spirit, a wisdom which was nothing other than the meaning of the crucifixion (2:7–10). Writing to the Romans Paul will conclude with a hymn to God praising God's mystery, kept secret in the past, now revealed, a mystery which is nothing other than the gospel Paul preaches (Rom 16:25–27; cf. also Col 1:26–27). In all of these texts Paul basically insists on the presence of Christ in the past. Apparently for Paul the revelation of Christ now is not the creation of something totally new but the manifestation of what was already there in a hidden way. Paul here could be saying that Christ was present at the exodus, but in a hidden and mysterious way, which only now to the eyes of faith can be understood.

Although Paul does not make this connection explicit, the reference to the "spiritual food" and "spiritual drink" could well be Paul's allusion to the Lord's supper, just as Paul explicitly connected the cloud and the sea with baptism. In the very next section Paul will deal explicitly with the cup and the bread of the Christian liturgy (10:16–17). And in the use of the Exodus story Paul here goes out of his way to connect both the food and the drink which sustained the Israelites. In this way the word "spiritual" (*pneumatikos*) takes on the sense of "prophetic," connecting the elements of the Old Testament with the gospel. "Spiritual" means part of that mystery whereby the gifts of God in Christ are present and active in the past.

After dealing with the initiating and nourishing experiences of Israel, Paul now turns to the revolts and sins of Israel. He refers explicitly to a text of Exodus thirty-two and then alludes to stories in Numbers twenty-five and twenty-one.

In the story of the golden calf, Aaron built the statue and the people cried out, "This is your God, O Israel who brought you out of the land of Egypt." The text continues,

> On seeing this, Aaron built an altar before the calf and pro-claimed, "Tomorrow is the feast of the Lord." Early the next day the people offered holocausts and brought peace offer-ings. Then they sat down to eat and drink, and rose up to revel. (Ex 32:5–6)

The story continues with God threatening to destroy all of Israel (Ex 32:7–14) and eventually having Moses slay some three thousand (Ex 32:28). The sin of the Israelites was not so much an abandonment of Yahweh, but rather a desire to worship him in the Canaanite fashion with images of snakes and bulls, much like the image Jeroboam later used in his northern temples to Yahweh (cf. 1 Kgs 12:26–32). Paul inter-prets the sin of Israel as pure and simple idolatry (10:7).

Numbers 25:1–9 tells the story of the Israelites at Moab where they sinned by worshiping Baal of Peor and having illicit sex with the Moabite women. God's anger flared against Israel and ordered public executions. Eventually, "the slaughter of the Israelites was checked; but only after twenty-four thousand had died." Although the number of casualties is bit off, Paul seems to be referring to his mention of the "twenty-three thousand" deaths in a single day (10:8). Paul, however, interprets this story, simply, as a warning against "sexual immorality."

Finally Paul alludes to the story in Numbers 21:4–9, where the Israelites rejected the manna as "wretched food" and were punished by poisonous snakes, from which "many died." The story in Numbers continues with God relenting and restoring the people through the image of a bronze serpent, the part of the story that the Fourth Gospel likes (cf. Jn 3:14–15). Paul, however, focuses only on the sin and punishment and likens it to "the destroyer" of God who kills the first born of Egypt (Ex 12:23). Paul also alludes again to the mysterious presence of Christ in the desert of the exodus, a mystery that unites "us" with "them": "Let us not test Christ as some of them did" (10:9).

In all these gruesome stories—which Paul rather likes—we see the prophetic theme of God as destroyer. For a group of people who fail morally, the presence of God is dangerous. The holiness of God is a blessing only for those who are holy. It is a disaster for those who are not (cf. Is 6:1–7). The nearness of God brings serious consequences. God must not be trivialized.

Paul states clearly, nothing has changed in this matter. These stories are "examples" (*typoi*) for us (10:6, 11). This word carries very much the same weight as "spiritual," in that both expressions underline the prophetic character of the stories, the way these stories describe present realities, not just things of the past.

All the more, Paul states, should these stories speak to us "upon whom the end of the ages has come" (10:11), upon whom God is about to manifest his holy presence. The Corinthians seem to understand the "spiritual" and eschatological character of their community. All the more should they see the urgency of holiness in conduct. All the more should they sense the importance of moral life. Although Paul may have composed these scriptural reflections for another community, he knows they apply to the Corinthians.

84

The last verses (10:12–13) express a balancing although obscure thought. Trials like these look tough on the human level. Our faith must rise to picture a "faithful" God behind these, who gives both strength and a "way out."

For reflection. Why is Paul telling his readers to consider these Old Testament pictures of an angry God? Today we frequently use Old Testament texts describing the salvation of God, as Paul did in the beginning of this section. But we tend to relegate the texts of God's anger and punishment to those parts which somehow no longer apply to people of the New Testament.

The prophets spent a lot of time preaching on the anger of God. They did it to insist on the seriousness of sin. Sin affects the very principle of the universe. Sin consists of the radical capacity to destroy ourselves. Any gift of salvation does not mean much if we do not have a sense of sin. The point of the whole section in fact is summed up by Paul, "Therefore whoever thinks he is standing secure should take care not to fall" (10:12).

The God described in these angry and punishing stories is the same God we worship as the loving Father of Jesus. God is the same. And for God there is no time span between the Old Testament events, the time of Paul, and our time. In and through God's eternity, these stories of the past become powerful "examples" for us.

The Lord's Supper and Avoiding Idolatry (10:14–22)

The Corinthians' nearness to God is dramatized by their participation in the Lord's Supper, a topic Paul intends to treat more thoroughly in the next main section of this letter (cf. 11:2–13). Just as the Israelites ate the "spiritual food" and drank the "spiritual drink" flowing from Christ (10:3–4), so the Corinthians "participate" in the blood and body of Christ by the cup and bread of the Lord's supper.

¹⁴Therefore, my beloved, avoid idolatry. ¹⁵I am speaking as to a sensible people; judge for yourselves what I am saying. ¹⁶The cup of blessing that we bless, is it not a participation in the blood of Christ? The bread that we break, is it not a participation in the body of Christ? ¹⁷Because the loaf of bread is one, we though many, are one body, for we all partake of the one loaf.

¹⁸Look at Israel according to the flesh; are not those who eat the sacrifices participants in the altar? ¹⁹So what am I saying? That meat sacrificed to idols is anything? Or that an idol is anything? ²⁰No, I mean that what they sacrifice, [they sacrifice] to demons, not to God, and I do not want you to become participants with demons. ²¹You cannot drink the cup of the Lord and also the cup of demons. You cannot partake of the table of the Lord and of the table of demons. ²²Or are we provoking the Lord to jealous anger? Are we stronger than he?

Paul's allusion to the Lord's Supper ("the cup of blessing" and "the bread we break") expresses an interesting interpretation of this ritual, which was modeled on Jesus' last supper (Mt 26:26–35; Mk 14:22–31; Lk 22:14–38) and quickly became a liturgical service in the Christian community. Here Paul sees this table fellowship as a "participation" (*koinonia*) in the blood and body of Christ. The special mention of the Christ's blood refers to his death. Paul is speaking of the Lord's Supper as a way of being part of the death of Jesus. The gospel descriptions of the last supper—already described as ritualized—do not clearly contain this interpretation. Paul knew of mystery cults in his day where one took part in sacred dramas to participate in the life (and sometimes death) of the gods. Paul also knew of sacred meals which were supposed to draw people closer to the gods. This interpretation of the Lord's Supper ritual might be in fact an example of early Christian writers drawing on their cultural world to understand their faith.

On the other hand Paul reinforces this participatory interpretation by referring apparently to the "peace offerings" in the

Temple cult, where the animal sacrificed was also served for dinner (Lv 7:11–21). "Are not those who eat the sacrifices participants (*koinonoi*) in the altar?" (10:18). He expects the Corinthians to understand this and be able to draw from it the important conclusion that is the real point of the instruction.

Before developing the logic of this thought, Paul adds an essential corollary. "Because the loaf of bread is one, we, though many are one body, for we all partake of the one loaf" (10:17). He will develop this thought in the next chapter where he deals with abuses at the Lord's supper. The important thing here is to see the natural flip from considering the "body of Christ" in which we participate by the bread—what we today call the eucharistic body of Christ—and "the body" which describes the community—what we today call the mystical body of Christ.

The real point of the instruction—as part of this letter to Corinth—brings Paul back to the question of meat offered to idols. You cannot participate in the holy things of God and then participate in cults connected with evil. Any form of idolatry is wrong because you are holy. This is the same reasoning Paul used regarding abstaining from sexual evil (6:15–20).

While Paul sees idols as illusions, nothing but hunks of wood and metal, he is not so sanguine about "demons" (*daimonioi*). While originally referring to deities or gods, this term in Jewish apocalyptic imagery described powerful evil spirits (cf. Rv 16:14) and agents of the devil (cf. Mt 12:24). As immersed in this Jewish apocalyptic view, Paul—as well as Jesus—saw evil as more than human. Evil was a force in the world that could enslave humans, a force which only God can destroy. To play around with the symbols of evil, like idols, was to expose oneself dangerously close to this evil force.

The last point in this section (10:22), however, shifts away from the apocalyptic perspective to the traditional prophetic perspective of God himself as the danger. God deals with sin. God is not a detached or abstract energy source. God is a jealous God.

For reflection. Paul here describes Christian life as part of a bigger picture. He describes the options of participating in the body and blood of Christ or participating in demons. He describes cult or liturgy as bringing us into this bigger picture, symbolized here by "the cup" and "the table" (10:21). The bigger picture of Christian cult is double: first, we are offered the possibility of being part of the cup and table "of the Lord" and secondly, we are offered the possibility of being part of the body of all who "partake of the one loaf."

Our faith thus brings solidarity. Forces in our culture entice us and pressure us into evil solidarities. A retailer feels the pressure of competition to buy clothing made from "sweat shops." And those cheap prices entice us to make the final purchase of that clothing. But our faith says we need not stand alone. We share the power of the body of Christ. Christian liturgy is a wellspring of that power in solidarity.

Meat Offered to Idols, Continued (10:23–11:1)

After several digressions Paul returns to the topic that began this section, meat offered to the idols and the Corinthian "enlightened" attitude that justified their disregard of the issue. Paul starts with a statement of the imaginary conversation partner he was talking to in chapter 8:

> [23]"Everything is lawful," but not everything is beneficial. "Everything is lawful," but not everything builds up. [24]No one should seek his own advantage, but that of his neighbor. [25]Eat anything sold in the market, without raising questions on grounds of conscience, [26]for "the earth and its fullness are the Lord's." [27]If an unbeliever invites you and you want to go, eat whatever is placed before you, without raising questions on the grounds of conscience. [28]But if someone says to you, "This was offered in sacrifice," do not eat it on account of the one who called attention to it and on account of conscience; [29]I mean not your own conscience, but the other's. For why

should my freedom be determined by someone else's conscience? ³⁰If I partake thankfully, why am I reviled for that over which I give thanks?

³¹So whether you eat or drink, or whatever you do, do everything for the glory of God. ³²Avoid giving offense, whether to Jews or Greeks or the church of God, ³³just as I try to please everyone in every way, not seeking my own benefit but that of the many, that they may be saved.

¹Be imitators of me, as I am of Christ.

Paul gets down to very specific cases in order to illustrate his general principle: give up some your rights in order not to hurt another. If you don't know, don't ask. Use the ambiguity of the situation. But if someone is checking you out, if someone would be led to think you are an idolater, give up your right to eat meat. Seek not your own benefit, but that of the many. In this way you become part of the drama of their salvation (10:33).

The expression "church of God" here (10:32) as parallel to "Jews or Greeks" looks very much like an all encompassing reality, not just the Christian assembly of a city like Corinth (cf. 1:2). In the way he developed connections among the churches, Paul must have thought of "the"church in some universal sense. On the other hand Paul knew of no world organization of churches or any hierarchical network. The closest parallel to Paul's sense of universal church would be the Jewish people as a whole, spread around the world. They recognized that they were one people, even though there was no world Jewish organization.

As a final thought to this whole section on Christian conduct, Paul adds the idea of "imitation." Paul, who sets aside his rights as an apostle for the sake of others (9:1–23), who tries "to please everyone in every way," is a model. Earlier in the letter writing about his actions as the "foolish" apostle, he told his readers to imitate him (4:16). Here he makes clear that he is not the ultimate model, "Be imitators of me, as I am of Christ." His life can be a guide to others only as it reflects Christ. Clearly Christ is the model of one who gave up his rights for our salvation.

For reflection. What is Paul saying here? Trying to please everyone in every way sounds either like acting like a sycophant or rejecting any radical or revolutionary decision. Jesus did not please everyone. Is Paul thinking only about "the weak"? In what contemporary issues would Paul's ethical principle apply well? Where would it seem to be wrong to apply? We speak today a great deal about being our own person. How then can the theme of "imitation," even the "imitation of Christ" provide an attractive approach to life?

VI

Problems at Church
Decorum and Unity
(11:2–34)

In this later part of the letter Paul turns his attention to the prayer assembly of the Corinthian and deals with a series of problems. The first deals with the proper dress of men and women; the second, with the proper behavior eating at the memorial of Jesus' last supper. The first starts with a praise; the second, with a reproach.

Men and Women at Church (11:2–16)

The first of these instructions focuses on the ritual of prophecy, a ritual in which obviously both men and women were active:

> [2]I praise you because you remember me in everything and hold fast to the traditions, just as I handed them on to you.
>
> [3]But I want you to know that Christ is the head of every man, and a husband the head of his wife, and God the head of Christ. [4]Any man who prays or prophesies with his head covered brings shame upon his head. [5]But any woman who prays or prophesies with her head unveiled brings shame upon her head, for it is one and the same thing as if she had her head shaved. [6]For if a woman does not have her head veiled, she may as well have her hair cut off. But if it is shameful for a woman to have her hair cut off or her head shaved, then she should wear a veil.
>
> [7]A man, on the other hand, should not cover his head, because he is the image and glory of God, but a woman is the

glory of man. [8]For a man did not come from woman, but woman from man; [9]nor was man created for woman, but woman for man; [10]for this reason a woman should have a sign of authority on her head, because of the angels. [11]Woman is not independent of man or man of woman in the Lord. [12]For just as woman came from man, so man is born of woman; but all things are from God.

[13]Judge for yourselves: is it proper for a woman to pray to God with her head unveiled? [14]Does not nature itself teach you that if a man wears his hair long it is a disgrace to him, [15]whereas if a woman has long hair it is her glory, because long hair has been given [her] for a covering? [16]But if anyone is inclined to be argumentative, we do not have such a custom, nor do the churches of God.

This is one of those texts in Paul many people would just as soon skip over. When he writes about short hair and long hair as a "teaching of nature," Paul shows his ignorance of history and cultures. When he speaks of "woman coming from man" and "woman created for man," he shows his fundamentalist interpretation of Genesis two. When he insists on men looking like men and women looking like women at church, he contradicts the important principle which he will declare in a future letter, "For all of you who were baptized into Christ . . . there is neither Jew nor Greek, there is neither slave nor free person, there is neither male nor female; for you are all one in Christ Jesus" (Gal 3:27–28).

One way of handling these difficulties is to look on the positive side. Many of the presuppositions in this text contain important ideas about women in the early church. The most obvious and important presupposition is that women did prophesy. As we will see in the coming sections of this letter (cf. esp. 14:1–12), the prophet was an important person in the church. When Paul does bother to rank roles, he places prophets second only to apostles. Prophecy meant speaking in the name of God and provided a powerful thrust in the building up of the church.

Another positive presupposition lies in the way Paul's statements are about mutual dependence among men and women (11:11–12). Focusing on this interdependence is a way of overcoming the fruitless preoccupation about who is more important than whom.

The Greco-Roman world was preoccupied about hierarchy, about a kind of ladder of importance where differences were seen in terms of more or less. This view is rooted in the philosophy of neo-Platonism where the diversity of the universe could be reconciled with the unity of its source by seeing the diversity as simply the progressive limitation of being. One kind of thing is different from another kind because it has everything the other has and more. In this view the higher reality does not really need the lower because it has all the functions of the lower—and more.

On the other hand, insistence on mutual dependence over hierarchy stresses far more something like harmony, where difference augments the beauty of each note. One cannot have great power over another if one depends on the other. At a minimum basic self-interest dictates cooperation among interdependent people. At a higher level, love rejoices in the richness of diversity in connectedness. Paul stresses the harmony of this interdependence by a reference to God. "All things are from God" (11:12).

Along the lines of this mutuality of the sexes, Paul does in fact give instructions to both men and women—although he says much nicer things about men. By giving instructions to both, Paul in effect is arguing that men should look like men and women like women. He does not like the unisex look. Why is this difference in dress, at least in church, a big deal? At this point we can only guess, but a good possibility was the prevalence of homosexual love in Greece and the Jewish abhorrence of homosexuality (cf. Lv 18:22; 20:13). At the time of Paul, "Greek love" was the euphemism for homosexual acts.

Obviously the social conventions of the day led Paul to prescribe the "head covering" or veil for the woman and not for the man. The propriety here might have had some sexual significance also. A woman prepared for sex by letting her long trusses flow down over her shoulders. Some prostitutes also advertised for business by displaying their hair.

Nevertheless Paul presents his teaching in the context of some superiority of man over woman. He describes the husband as the *head* of the wife. And if there is any doubt about what it means, Paul describes Christ as the *head* of a man, and God as the *head* of Christ (11:3). Despite the text of Genesis 1:27, Paul seems to limit being an "image" (*eikon*) of God to the male human (11:7), suggesting that the female human gets a share in this image by being a "reflection" (*doxa*) of the male (11:7).

What the "sign of authority" consists of and what "the angels" have to do with this matter (11:10) remains a puzzle for us today. From the context, we would expect Paul to require a "sign of subordination" on the head of a woman. What is this "sign of authority"? Could it be the woman's authority, for example, to prophesy? Perhaps in the ancient Near-Eastern mind and not so ancient Near-Eastern mind, the veil on a woman gives her "authority," for instance to go where she wants. Without that veil she is subject to shameful ridicule, with the veil she has a freedom to do what she wants.

Why are "angels" mentioned here by Paul—without any explanation? "The angels" in the New Testament mind are not human beings. (Later church writers would suggest Paul is referring to bishops!) In the Bible they are divine-like messengers between God and humanity. Thus "fallen angels," like those in Genesis 6:11, are generally not called "angels" (except in Rv 12:7 and Jude 6). Paul refers to the Law being given through an angel (Gal 3:19). In Jewish legends and in some writings of the Bible, angels were sort of guardians of the natural order and also guardians of cities and communities (Rv 1:20). In the Book of Revelation we hear of an angel mediating the prayers of the holy ones to God (Rv 8:3–4), as well as forming the core group of the heavenly liturgy (Rv 4:9; cf. Lk 2:3; Is 6:2–3). Perhaps following

94

the suggestion of Psalm 138:1, Paul pictures the human gathering of believers as church sharing in the heavenly liturgy, where angels are present. A few centuries later, Christians would introduce the liturgical chant, "Holy, holy, holy" with an invitation to pray, "therefore with the angels and archangels. . . ." Whatever the meaning of his references here, Paul drops the topic without explanation.

A certain grumpiness in Paul shows up in the last verse. Appealing to practice in "the churches of God" (11:16), he pulls the plug on further discussion—an easy trap that people in authority can fall into.

For reflection. Many Christians of the Southern Baptist traditions see this section of Paul as binding *point by point* on their marriages. After all, scripture—even the parts we do not like—is supposed to binding on us. Other Christians can disregard these texts without sensing any highhandedness over scripture. What are the issues here?

Paul's description of the superiority of husband over wife was the prevailing social view of his day. Paul was rather conservative from the social and political point of view. His advice earlier in this letter was for Christians to remain in the same marital and social state they happened to be in since this age was rapidly coming to an end (7:17–31).

If Paul were speaking to the prevailing social view of our day, what would he say? How do we determine what in Paul's *letter* is social medium and what is binding message?

One thing is clear, however, the Corinthian church and Paul—despite the prevailing social view of the day—accepted both men and women exercising prophecy in the church. We do not have many examples of women prophets from the Old Testament. The example of Hulda (2 Kgs 22:14–20) comes to mind, but this text never appears in the liturgical readings. To prevent any person from exercising his or her gift in the church is to lose part of the richness which God wants for the church.

The Lord's Supper—Problems (11:17–22)

In the second of these instructions, the one where he starts with a reproach, Paul focuses on the Lord's Supper:

> [17]In giving this instruction, I do not praise the fact that your meetings are doing more harm than good. [18]First of all, I hear that when you meet as a church there are divisions among you, and to a degree I believe it; [19]there have to be factions among you in order that (also) those who are approved among you may become known. [20]When you meet in one place, then it is not to eat the Lord's supper, [21]for in eating, each one goes ahead with his own supper, and one goes hungry while another gets drunk. [22]Do you not have houses in which you can eat and drink? Or do you show contempt for the church of God and make those who have nothing feel ashamed? What can I say to you? Shall I praise you? In this matter I do not praise you.

Paul here sounds something like the prophet Amos. Eight centuries earlier than Paul during a time of material prosperity, this prophet spoke in the name of God describing the solemn liturgies of the Israelites:

> I hate, I spurn your feasts, I take no pleasure in your
>   solemnities;
> Your cereal offerings I will not accept, nor consider your
>   stall-fed peace offerings.
> Away with your noisy songs! I will not listen to the melodies
>   of your harps.
> But if you would offer me holocausts, then let justice surge
>   like water, and goodness like an unfailing stream.
>   (Am 5:21–24)

Throughout most of the Old Testament prophets can be found with this theme: the temple worship of God is worthless without a just and ethical treatment of other human beings.

The religious event Paul is speaking of is "the Lord's supper" (*kyriakon deipnon*, 11:20). This is the first time we hear this term for the ritual which quickly became the principal liturgy among Christians. The Greek word, *deipnon*, indicates a big meal, much like the "last supper" of Jesus. For Christians at this time, the ritual was truly "the Lord's dinner."

For Paul at Corinth the ethical problem is not so much the exploitation of the poor, as it was for Amos, but simply the neglect of the poor, and precisely in the church of God. Paul writes of "divisions" and "factions," as he mentioned in the first part of this letter (cf. 1:10–16). In this part of the letter we learn that the factions are around those who go hungry and those who get too much (11:21). The "divisions" thus appear to be along the lines of the social strata so important in the Greco-Roman world, dividing the rich and the poor.

Without developing the elaborate images of divine rejection of such worship as did Amos, Paul simply says, "Your meetings are doing more harm than good" (11:17).

It is interesting to see how Paul describes the problem. He makes two parallel contrasts. One is between "the Lord's supper" and each one's "own supper" (11:20–21). The second is between "the church of God" and "houses which you have" (11:22). Of course "the church of God" took place in somebody's house, like the house of Gaius, host of the whole Corinthian church (Rom 16:23). The church was not a separate building. The transformation of somebody's house into "the church of God" occurred precisely in the hosting of "the Lord's supper." Eating and drinking simply to satisfy hunger was appropriate in one's own house (cf. also 11:34). But during the "Lord's supper," while one was in the "church of God," other priorities prevailed. In effect, one sat at table as the guest of the Lord, and any offensive divisions—especially those between the rich and the poor—was an act of contempt to the Lord bringing us together.

For reflection. Has the problem of divisions between the rich and the poor within the church ever been solved? Now that we have dedicated church buildings, probably none of us feels the temptation to make ourselves at home to the exclusion of people from the other side of town. But where are the people from the other side of town?

Eventually the large numbers that came into the church seemed to have made the logistics of a main meal too difficult for celebrating the Lord's Supper; hence, we moved to the "chip" and "sip" forms of eucharist. There may be strengths and weaknesses in this shift. Can you see each? What should "table fellowship with the Lord" always mean?

The Recall of the Gospel Tradition (11:23–26)

Paul interrupts this prophetic challenge of his readers to recall the tradition which described the Last Supper:

> [23]For I received from the Lord what I also handed on to you, that the Lord Jesus, on the night he was handed over, took bread, [24]and, after he had given thanks, broke it and said, "This is my body that is for you. Do this in remembrance of me." [25]In the same way also the cup, after supper, saying, "This cup is the new covenant in my blood. Do this as often as you drink it, in remembrance of me." [26]For as often as you eat this bread and drink the cup, you proclaim the death of the Lord until he comes.

The opening words, "I received from . . . what I also handed on to you," appear to be almost technical terms at the time of Paul to signal a piece of oral tradition by which the Christians passed on to one another the stories of Jesus essential to their faith (cf. also 15:3). Decades after Paul these oral traditions would be collected and written also in the gospels. The tradition Paul describes here will be repeated in the eighties in very similar words by Luke in his gospel (Lk 22:15–20). A somewhat differently worded tradition will be written down in the late sixties and in the eighties by Mark and Matthew (Mk 14:22–25; Mt 26:26–29). The similarities and differences can be seen in the very words of Jesus, first over the bread:

Paul: "This is my body that is for you. Do this in remembrance of me" (1 Cor 11:24).

Luke: "This is my body, which will be given for you; do this in memory of me" (22:19).

Mark: "Take it; this is my body" (14:22).

Matthew: "Take and eat; this is my body" (26:26).

Similarly, Jesus' words over the wine:

Paul: "This cup is the new covenant in my blood. Do this as often as you drink it, in remembrance of me" (1 Cor 11:25).

Luke: "This cup is the new covenant in my blood, which will be shed for you" (22:20).

Mark: "This is my blood of the covenant, which will be shed for many" (14:24).

Matthew: "Drink from it, all of you, for this is my blood of the covenant, which will be shed on behalf of many for the forgiveness of sins" (26:27–28).

In each addition of a word or phrase we see a special understanding or interpretation brought out.

In this text of Paul, we have by far the earliest written form of this tradition. Here Paul around A.D. 55 is reminding the Corinthians of his preaching around A.D. 52, a preaching which had already become a tradition in the church. The insistence by Paul here and later by Luke on the command to "do this in memory of me" shows how quickly the Christians did in fact see the Last Supper of Jesus as a ritual by which they could truly become church. All the verbal forms of this tradition, including that in Mark and Matthew, focused on the opening breaking of the bread and the concluding cup of wine, without any mention of the rest of the meal. This simplification again suggests a ritualization.

Paul says he received this tradition "from the Lord." More than likely, Paul learned of this tradition through the Christians he lived with after his call and conversion. Among the Christians this ritual was a living tradition, linking the church with the historical Jesus on the night before he died and the risen Lord who really continued to host his Supper. In effect receiving the tradition from the living practice of the church was receiving it "from the Lord."

In the Pauline tradition, the broken bread is identified with Christ's "body that is for you." The word "body" refers to the concrete reality of Jesus, perhaps with a nuance of being subject to some action or influence. The expression "for you" suggests the redemptive and vicarious character of that body. The reality is "on our behalf" and "for our benefit." Luke later will include the word "given" (Lk 22:19), emphasizing even more this redemptive and vicarious character.

In the Pauline tradition the words over the wine cup identify it as "the cup of the new covenant in my blood." The particular combination, bread and wine, as analogues to body and blood, had not yet arisen. For Paul, as for Luke, the combination is the bread and the cup as analogues to the body and the new covenant. Perhaps Paul and Luke name the cup as standing for its contents, the wine. And for both Paul and Luke the new covenant is specifically described as "in my blood." Thus the development of the symmetry of the Mark-Matthew tradition is easy to understand. However, the earlier Paul-Luke tradition stays closer to the picture of two separated actions as part of a larger meal, the breaking of the bread to begin the meal and the passing of a blessing cup to end the meal. Both Paul and Luke describe the action with the cup as "after supper." In Paul and Luke the stress is less on the parallel "elements" of the ritual than on the separate actions which evoke the expiatory death of Jesus and the establishment of a "new covenant."

Earlier in the letter Paul had given a meaning to the Lord's Supper as a participation in the blood and body of Christ, that is participating in Christ's death (10:16). Here Paul speaks of eating the bread and drinking from the cup as "proclaiming the death of the Lord" (11:26). Clearly the death of the Lord was in some mysterious way present in the ritualized Lord's Supper at Corinth and elsewhere. Those who participated as the church of God in this ritual proclaimed by their action and lives the very death of Christ without saying a word. That death was present in their daily lives.

Moreover, this death brings about the "new covenant." Jesus' blood is like "the blood of the covenant" mentioned in Exodus 24:8. Just as Moses ratified Israel's covenant with God by the "communion sacrifices" and sprinkled the blood of these sacrifices on the people to dramatize and actualize their participation in the covenant (Ex 24:3–11), so the blood of Jesus as part of a new communion sacrifice brings about a new covenant. A new relationship with God arises from the death of Jesus on the cross. Now this new relationship is dramatized and actualized by the Lord's supper.

Paul again will refer to the "new covenant" in Second Corinthians 3:6, where he clearly draws on the text of Jeremiah 31:31, the only place in the Old Testament where the expression "new covenant" is mentioned. In Jeremiah and in Second Corinthians the newness does not consist so much in the replacement of the old covenant, but in the new way in which that Sinai covenant can exist in the heart of the believer and thus bring about a spiritual transformation.

For reflection. What does the eucharist mean to me? What does church mean to me? We have this sacred contact with the death of Jesus because a church understood and lived this tradition, passing it down through the centuries to our days, to our churches. We receive the same bread and cup—becoming part of the death of Jesus—and proclaim this death to the world—without saying a word. Churches of the future need to receive this tradition and continue the proclamation—until the Lord comes. Who will pass this tradition of faith on?

The Lord's Supper—Problems Continued (11:27-33)

Now Paul turns back to the problems at Corinth and warns the Corinthians of the seriousness of their failings. In the A-B-A' composition of the whole section on the Lord's Supper (11:17-33), these verses link back to 11:17-22.

> [27]Therefore whoever eats the bread or drinks the cup of the Lord unworthily will have to answer for the body and blood of the Lord. [28]A person should examine himself, and so eat the bread and drink the cup. [29]For anyone who eats and drinks without discerning the body, eats and drinks judgment on himself. [30]That is why many among you are ill and infirm, and a considerable number are dying. [31]If we discerned ourselves, we would not be under judgment; [32]but since we are judged by (the) Lord, we are being disciplined so that we may not be condemned along with the world.
>
> [33]Therefore, my brothers, when you come together to eat, wait for one another. [34]If anyone is hungry, he should eat at home, so that your meetings may not result in judgment. The other matters I shall set in order when I come.

The problem is that of disunity and disrespect for the poor in the assembly. When Paul speaks of eating the bread or drinking the cup unworthily, he has in mind this problem of the congregation, this problem of how Christians at the ritual relate to one another. Almost for sure, then, when Paul challenges his readers to "discern the body" (11:29), he is referring to the congregation, which is "one body" because it partakes of "the one loaf" (10:17). The sudden shift from the bread and wine to the congregation is a bit confusing, but it should not surprise us. Paul made the same shift in the previous section of the letter (10:14-22) when he began speaking of the Lord's Supper. The "test" or "examination" required of each person as they eat the bread and drink the cup (11:28) is that they understand and live the social requirements of the eucharist. Those requirements are not lived when one eats his fill and another goes hungry at the Lord's Supper. Those requirements are not lived when we approach the Lord's Supper with the attitudes leading us to grab simply to satisfy our hungry appetites.

Catholic scholars have frequently seen in the challenge "discern the body" an expression of faith in the Real Presence of Jesus in the bread and wine. Taken out of context the wording here would work for such an interpretation. In the context of the letter, however, this interpretation poses the problem of why Paul would suddenly hold out acceptance of a doctrinal formulation of faith as the criterion for participating at the Lord's Supper.

Nevertheless, the realism of Paul's understanding is an important step in the later development of this doctrine of Real Presence. The unworthy eating and drinking at the Lord's Supper makes one "answerable" in the sense of becoming one who has offended (*enochos*) the body and blood of Christ (11:27). The combination of "body and blood" designates the historical Jesus in his act of dying. This historical act therefore is somehow present at the Lord's Supper.

At the same time the sudden and ambiguous shift to "the body" which is the congregation (11:29) is almost a play on words. The historical dying body of Christ and the social body of Christians at the Lord's Supper are superimposed. The vagueness and ambiguity become the expression of the mysterious identification of the congregation with Christ.

Paul tries to drive home the seriousness of offending the body and blood of Christ by linking up the sufferings of the community at Corinth with this sin (11:30–32). The theme is from the classical prophets: God punishes sin. Suffering and misfortune can be God's discipline. Pushing this theme too much leads to the problem of Job.

For reflection. What do we stress as the conditions for a worthy "eating the bread and drinking the cup of the Lord"? Do the rituals in our church for eucharist or communion service provide for a moment of "discerning the body" the way Paul was concerned about it? How many ways is Christ "present" at eucharist?

VII

The Spiritual Gifts
(12:1—14:40)

Another question comes up, "Now in regard to . . ." The question must have dealt with the various functions and activities at a Christian assembly, functions and activities, seen as gifts of the Holy Spirit. Paul refers to these functions and activities by two words, "spiritual things" (*pneumatika*, 12:1) or "gifts" (*charismata*, 12:4). With this topic we get to the heart of the problems at Corinth. Paul had these "spiritual gifts" in mind when he started the letter. He mentioned them in his opening prayer as he searched for something to thank God for (cf. 1:5–7).

Unity and Variety among the Gifts (12:1–11)

For Paul understanding the Holy Spirit is the key to understanding the variety of spiritual gifts in the church:

> ¹Now in regard to spiritual gifts, brothers, I do not want you to be unaware. ²You know how, when you were pagans, you were constantly led and carried away to mute idols. ³Therefore, I tell you that nobody speaking by the spirit of God says, "Jesus be accursed." And no one can say "Jesus is Lord," except by the Holy Spirit.
> ⁴There are different kinds of spiritual gifts but the same Spirit; ⁵there are different forms of service but the same Lord; ⁶there are different workings but the same God who produces all of them in everyone. ⁷To each individual the manifestation of the Spirit is given for some benefit. ⁸To one is given through the Spirit the expression of wisdom; to another the

expression of knowledge according to the same Spirit; [9]to another faith by the same Spirit; to another gifts of healing by the one Spirit; [10]to another mighty deeds; to another prophecy; to another discernment of spirits; to another varieties of tongues; to another interpretation of tongues. [11]But one and the same Spirit produces all of them, distributing them individually to each person as he wishes.

Paul starts with an implied contrast (12:2–3). He describes the former "pagan" condition as being driven and carried away in their religious activity, a kind of mindless mode which "pagan" writers admitted and admired. They called it "enthusiasm." (The NAB is less emphatic than the Greek about the passive nature of this involvement. The Greek says: "constantly attracted and led away.") Paul is preparing his readers for a role of the Christian Spirit as one which in contrast is not so "enthusiastic," one which remains ordered and rational. Thus Paul describes the characteristic of the Holy Spirit as simply the ability to confess, "Jesus is Lord." This expression apparently was a very well-known credal statement (cf. Rom 10:9).

The order and harmony of the gifts is rooted above all in the unified source of all the gifts. Paul says this three times in triple synonymous parallelism, working through the three names we now associate with the Trinity:

- There are different gifts (*charismata*) but the same Spirit (*pneuma*).

- There are different services (*diakoniai*) but the same Lord (*kyrios*).

- There are different energies (*energemata*) but the same God (*theos*).

We see in this parallelism three words to describe the "spiritual gifts." The first, "gifts," stresses the unmerited and perhaps unpredictable character. This aspect is associated with the Spirit of God. In the Old Testament, the Spirit was the personification of the free and surprising power of God. The second name, "services," stresses the down to earth and ecclesial character of the gifts. The Greek word is rooted in the sense of preparing a meal (cf. Lk 10:40), but it quickly becomes the foundation concept for the office of "deacon" (cf. Phil 1:1). This aspect is associated with Jesus, the one whom Paul consistently names with the expression "the Lord" (except when he is citing an Old Testament passage). The third name, "energies" in the Greek, stresses the powerful and even miraculous character of the gifts. (The NAB translation "workings" does not quite cut it.) This aspect is associated with God the Father, the one whom Paul consistently names with the word "God."

If the first part of the triple parallelism consists of virtual synonyms, what about the second part of the triple parallelism? Are the three names in the second part also synonymous? Probably not. Paul clearly distinguishes Jesus from the Father, and he never identifies the Spirit with Jesus, despite frequent misunderstandings of Second Corinthians 3:17 where Paul writes, "The Lord is the Spirit." (In that Second Corinthians text, "the Lord" is linked to an Old Testament citation naming Yahweh.) However, by placing "the Spirit," "the Lord," and "[the] God" in this parallel structure, Paul tightly associates all three with each other. A similar parallel occurs at Second Corinthians 13:13: "The grace of the Lord Jesus Christ and the love of God and the fellowship of the Holy Spirit be with you all." Later Christian theology will use these texts as springboards to develop the concept of the Trinity.

What Paul is stressing here is the unity of the spiritual gifts. The gifts, as we will see, may be manifold. However, if they are all rooted in a divine unity—no matter how you look on the gifts—then they must form a powerful harmony all working for a common end, "for some benefit."

Paul then gives a first listing of the community's gifts:

- "the expression of wisdom" (*logos sophias*)

- "the expression of knowledge" (*logos gnoseos*)

- "faith,"

- "healing,"

- "mighty deeds,"

- "prophecy,"

- "discernment of spirits,"

- "variety of tongues,"

- "interpretation of tongues."

In the prayer opening this letter (cf. 1:3–9), Paul thanked God for the gifts of "words" (*logos*) and "knowledge" (*gnosis*). Here Paul speaks of these activities as one gift, perhaps not really differing from "words of wisdom." "Faith" here must mean something other than the basic attitude of trust through which God's saving power comes (Rom 8:22; cf. 1 Cor 2:5; 15:14, 17; 16:13). As a special gift to some, this "faith" sounds much more like the power "to move mountains" (cf. Mt 17:20; 21:21 and par.). Thus "faith," "healing," and "mighty deeds" appear very similar. "Variety of tongues" is paired with "interpretation of tongues," since Paul sees both functions being performed by the same person, as he will explain later (cf. 14:13). More than likely, "prophecy" and "discernment of spirits" are also paired and appear to be two different aspects of the same gift, as Paul again explains later (cf. 14:29–32; 1 Thes 5:19–21).

After giving this list, Paul roots all the gifts in the "one and the same Spirit" (12:11). Therefore no conflict can exist among the gifts. If conflict here arises, we should suspect that the manifestations are not of the Holy Spirit. Paul stresses the freedom of the Spirit in the distribution of these gifts. Later, especially under the influence of Luke, the church will "domesticate" the Spirit, controlling this freedom by such human actions as the "laying on of hands" (cf. Acts 8:13; 19:6; 1 Tm 4:14; 2 Tm 1:6). In the letters he actually wrote, Paul never speaks of "laying on of hands." Therefore no sign would exist to divide *a priori* the faithful into those empowered and those not, into those with leadership roles and those without. Writing of marital states in the church, Paul said before, "Each has a particular gift from God" (1 Cor 7:7). Here Paul repeats the point. Concerning the spiritual gifts, it is the one and the same Spirit "distributing them individually to each person (*idia hekasto*) as he wishes" (12:11).

For reflection. What kind of a conversation can you imagine in heaven now between Luke and Paul about the role of the Spirit in the church? The church clearly developed in the span from the time of Paul (the sixties) to the time of Luke (the eighties). No one ever laments any lack in Paul's churches. These churches appear to be complete. As described in the Acts of the Apostles, the Lucan churches have several additional things like "presbyters" and "laying on of hands." We believe that the Holy Spirit guided that development.

Is there any reason to believe that the Holy Spirit stopped that guidance sometime after Luke? Major changes in the church continued into the second century A.D. What could that development during the formation of the New Testament and for sometime after mean in terms of options for development now? Probably out of respect for the sacred, we tend to freeze things. Could the New Testament itself give us courage to move in the line of supporting every single person in the church as a leader in his or her "spiritual expertise"?

The Church as the Body of Christ (12:12–31)

The harmony of diverse gifts appears in a brilliant metaphor Paul uses to describe the way differences can contribute to unity:

> [12]As a body is one though it has many parts, and all the parts of the body, though many, are one body, so also Christ.
> [13]For in one Spirit we were all baptized into one body,

whether Jews or Greeks, slaves or free persons, and we were all given to drink of one Spirit.

[14]Now the body is not a single part, but many. [15]If a foot should say, "Because I am not a hand I do not belong to the body," it does not for this reason belong any less to the body. [16]Or if an ear should say, "Because I am not an eye I do not belong to the body," it does not for this reason belong any less to the body. [17]If the whole body were an eye, where would the hearing be? If the whole body were hearing, where would the sense of smell be? [18]But as it is, God placed the parts, each one of them, in the body as he intended. [19]If they were all one part, where would the body be? [20]But as it is, there are many parts, yet one body. [21]The eye cannot say to the hand, "I do not need you," nor again the head to the feet, "I do not need you." [22]Indeed, the parts of the body that seem to be weaker are all the more necessary, [23]and those parts of the body that we consider less honorable we surround with greater honor, and our less presentable parts are treated with greater propriety, [24]whereas our more presentable parts do not need this. But God has so constructed the body as to give greater honor to a part that is without it, [25]so that there may be no division in the body, but that the parts may have the same concern for one another. [26]If (one) part suffers, all the parts suffer with it; if one part is honored, all the parts share its joy.

[27]Now you are Christ's body, and individually parts of it. [28]Some people God has designated in the church to be, first, apostles; second, prophets; third, teachers; then, mighty deeds; then gifts of healing, assistance, administration, and varieties of tongues. [29]Are all apostles? Are all prophets? Are all teachers? Do all work mighty deeds? [30]Do all have gifts of healing? Do all speak in tongues? Do all interpret? [31]Strive eagerly for the greatest spiritual gifts.

Greek writers contemporary with Paul used the word "body" (*soma*) to designate social entities. We do the same, as indicated in expressions like, "the student body," "the legislative body," etc. Paul picked up this use and by drawing attention to the physical analogue of this metaphor, he develops the theme of diversity in unity, the theme of organic unity. Not only does the diversity of organs in the body not harm unity, but actually supports it and is the essential condition for it.

A subtle originality, however, appears in Paul's use of this social metaphor. In the other Greek writers and in our normal use of the term "body" for a social entity, the body is basically the collection of the parts. A "student body" is the collection of all the students—along with the emotional glue and energy that each member contributes to the whole. The "student body" does not exist before the individuals are "incorporated" into that whole. When Paul says, however, "Now, you are Christ's body" (12:27), he is naming a reality that exists before the members are incorporated. Christ is already existing before the members become parts. All Christians are incorporated into, "baptized into" (Rom 6:3) Christ, into something greater than themselves. The functioning of this body and the roles of the members are designated by God (12:27).

By drawing attention to the physical analogue in this analysis Paul also (in an apparently original way) develops the theme of mutual dependence, the theme he began when speaking of the diversity of men and women in the church (cf. 7:11–12). Here he drives home the point. No part or organ of a body can say to another part "I do not need you" (12:21). No member of the church—no matter how honorable—can say to the others, "I do not need you." This intense interdependence is a clear rejection of the neo-Platonic explanation of diversity by way of hierarchical ladder of progressive limitations with a resulting relative independence of the higher over the lower.

This rejection of a hierarchy of honor also appears in Paul's tongue-in-cheek treatment of "the less presentable parts." Paul was very familiar with the hierarchy of honor. The public life of the government was filled with it. The clubs or voluntary associations of his day were full of it. Possibly the richer members of the Corinthian church, the ones who provided the essential material basis—like a place to meet or food to serve—expected some

111

symbols of honor within the church. In clubs those who provided the building to meet in were given the titles of "fathers" and "mothers" of the club, given elevated seats, and maybe fanned with ostrich feathers. But, as Paul says, watch the way people decorate their body. What parts get the most elaborate clothing? In the church, then, if anybody gets a lot of honor, do you know what that means about their functions? Is there some hierarchy or order in Paul's view of church? Certainly the ranks of "first," "second," and "third" found in his description of "apostles," "prophets," and "teachers" show some order or rank. As an apostle Paul certainly sees himself with authority over others. Later he will designate "the household of Stephanas" as one to which others should be "subordinate" (16:15–16). What Paul does *not* want is a hierarchy of honor.

All have a great gift from God and all perform a needed function in the Body. This is Paul's basic point. Our challenge is therefore to recognize our individual gifts. The worldly concern of comparing functions and feeling envy about another's role is a waste of energy. A hierarchy of honor is basically a system for the purpose of comparison and a system which fosters envy. This is a waste of the energy that should instead guide the parts to "have the same concern for one another" (12:25).

The list of member functions in the church parallels somewhat the list of gifts given earlier:

12:8–10	12:28–30
	apostles
prophecy, discernment of spirits	prophets
the expression of wisdom, the expression of knowledge	teachers
faith, healing, mighty deeds	healing
	assistance
	administration
variety of tongues	varieties of tongues
interpretation of tongues	interpreting

In the second list, besides including his own charism of being an apostle, Paul also here adds two other functions that would usually designate a person rich person in society. The wealthy heads of households provided "assistance" to the needy, especially if the needy were associated with their household. "Administration" was also a necessary skill for the wealthy heads of households and presupposed some form of assets to administer. Such wealthy people had their function in the church, more than likely as the local administrators and leaders of the community, the ones who could provide the logistics of the Lord's Supper.

Paul never speaks about who presided over the assemblies. It does not seem to have been an issue for him or for the Corinthians. However, serving a meal—whether in a small family or all the more to a fairly large group—requires someone to take charge. We know in Jewish families, the father of the family had this leadership role. We know also wealthy widows in Hellenistic families took over the role of the deceased husband both in the family and in the business. More than likely then the gifts of "assistance" and "administration" related to role of leading or presiding over the Lord's Supper. One of the major problems surfacing at Corinth appears to be the lack of good leadership. The body was suffering by the deficiency of some members. Thus in effect Paul is saying that wealth and social power should be considered an important gift of the Spirit to be used in the church for the concern for others.

For reflection. Should this organic unity—"if (one) part suffers, all the parts suffer with it; if one part is honored, all the parts share its joy" (12:26)—be the the test of our "corporate health" as a church? Do we suffer when we learn of the sufferings of other members or are we indifferent? Does the honor given to one member fill us with joy or envy?

Picture a church in which every member has a gift and function recognized by the congregation, in which no one envies the role of the other. Picture a church in which no one receives any greater honor—except for the special honors given to the weak—and no one seeks any greater honors. Picture the Body of Christ.

The Way of Love (12:31b–13:13)

Such an intense sense of concern for one another in the church is simply love for one another. If there is one gift of the Spirit that stands out—because it is all encompassing—that gift is love:

> 12:13bBut I shall show you a still more excellent way.

I

> 13:1If I speak in human and angelic tongues
>   but do not have love, I am a resounding gong
>   or a clashing cymbal.
> 2And if I have the gift of prophecy and comprehend all
>   mysteries and all knowledge;
> If I have faith so as to move mountains
>   but do not have love, I am nothing.
> 3If I give away everything I own, and if I hand my body
>   over so that I may boast
>   but do not have love, I gain nothing.

II

> 4Love is patient; love is kind.
> It is not jealous, (love) is not pompous, it is not inflated,
>   5it is not rude.
>   It does not seek its own interests, it is not
>   quick-tempered,
>   it does not brood over injury, 6it does not rejoice over
>   wrongdoing
> but rejoices with the truth
> 7It bears all things, believes all things, hopes all things,
>   endures all things.

III

> 8Love never fails.
>   If there are prophecies, they will be brought to
>   nothing;

114

If tongues, they will cease;
If knowledge, it will be brought to nothing.
⁹For we know partially and we prophesy partially,
    ¹⁰but when the perfect comes, the partial will pass
        away.
¹¹When I was a child, I used to talk as a child, think as
        a child, reason as a child;
    when I became a man, I put aside childish things.
¹²At present we see indistinctly, as in a mirror,
        but then face to face.
At present I know partially;
        then I shall know fully, as I am fully known.
¹³So faith, hope, love remain, these three; but the greatest
        of these is love.

Writing out this poem in verse allows us to see the parallelism, which is the heart of biblical poetry. The development of this poem consists not so much as an analysis of the parts or links to related ideas, but rather by multiple repetitions of the same idea with slightly different nuances or angles. Combining these different nuances and angles gives us an understanding of Paul's poetic theology.

The poem stands out in the letter, suggesting that it existed sometime beforehand. It could very well have been written by Paul earlier or written by someone close to Paul. The ideas and even some of the expressions are characteristic of Paul and his thought. Its place here in the letter underlines the importance of the unity and harmony of the church which Paul has been stressing.

Other letters of Paul contain poetic pieces. Mostly these compositions are praises or hymns to God (cf. Rom 11:33–36) or hymns to Christ (cf. Phil 2:6–11). As a praise or ode to a virtue, this poem in Corinthians is different.

It actually reminds us of the praises of Wisdom found in late Old Testament texts (cf. Wis 7:22–30). These praises of Wisdom are in fact praises of God, God's wisdom personified as a divine reality distinct from God. Paul's exuberance in praising

Love may stem from a sense of praising God. In the Old Testament texts, Wisdom dwells with human beings and enters into their lives (Wis 8:9–16; Prv 8:32–36). Wisdom in effect is a medium bonding humans to God. Paul here is clearing speaking about human beings "having" Love (13:1–3). More than likely Love here too is conceived as a divine-human reality, a medium by which human beings participate in a divine way of living.

The first stanza of the poem focuses on glorious actions of apparent godly persons and affirms Love as the core value of all these actions. Without this core value, they are nothing. The first two actions are "tongues" and "prophecy," the two spiritual gifts Paul is about to discuss in the next chapter. The description of "prophecy"as the comprehension of "all mysteries and all knowledge" (13:2), however, is a bit out of sync with the description of prophecy in the next chapter, where the action of the prophet is "building up, encouragement, and solace" (14:3).

The second stanza describes the qualities and characteristics of Love. The stanza starts with Love as "patient" and ends with Love which "endures all things." It also "bears all things" (13:3, 7). Paul stresses here how hard times and suffering are the test of Love. Sandwiched between two positive descriptions, are eight negations of bad actions. (In the Greek the eight negations are expressed with verbs, showing how Paul has personified Love.) The return to the positive aspects turns around the act of "rejoicing." Love "does not rejoice in wrongdoing but rejoices with the truth" (13:6). Love and joy are partners. The list of qualities and characteristics of Love here is somewhat parallel to the "fruit" of the Spirit which Paul lists in a later letter (Gal 5:22–23).

The third stanza describes the enduring and eschatological character of Love. Again Paul starts with prophecy and tongues to develop a contrast. The contrast with knowledge leads to a contrast between two epochs, the present epoch or world and the future epoch or world (13:9–12). Paul repeats the same contrast several times from different perspectives. It is a contrast between "the partial" and "the perfect" (*teleion*), between the "child" (*nepios*) and the "adult," between "the mirror" and "face to face." Paul is contrasting the present life with future eschatological life. We have seen his use of the same terms earlier to describe the Corinthians, either in terms of their spiritual possibilities (cf. *teleioi*, 2:6) or of their ethical deficiencies (cf. *nepioi*, 3:1). Paul builds his theology and ethics around the eschatological tension of the two epochs, but he sees that in some way the future epoch is present and available now through the Spirit and the Christian's participation in God's Love.

As inserted in Paul's letter to the Corinthians and specifically his teachings about the spiritual gifts, the ode to Love speaks volumes. Love is the core value of all the gifts. The words of wisdom, the miraculous healing, the spectacular prophecies mean nothing if they are not expressions of Love. If these gifts lead to strife and divisions within the church, something is horribly wrong. Furthermore, the permanence of Love contrasts with the temporary character of the other gifts. "Prophecy," "tongues," and "knowledge" will pass. The Corinthians have been focusing on their ecclesial functions to the extent that they have forgotten that the church belongs to this world, not the next. The church is only the beachhead of the Kingdom in this world. Any true church must be prepared to pass away and make room for the Kingdom.

For reflection. This ode to Love helps us understand the heart of Christian ethics. Paul will come back to that point writing to the Galatians. We could object, however, that such an ethic is impossible or leads to mousey passivity. How would Paul answer these objections?

Here this poem is directed to church life. In some parts it stands ready to accuse us of failures under the guise of doing great good, e.g., prophecy without love. Could this poem be directed to us today in some of our illusions of doing good?

Love here appears as the bond between this world and the next, helping us to understand the "childish things" of this

117

world and helping us root our hearts in the next. Can you think of an example of a deeply loving person who exemplifies these perspectives? Does that person show signs of an irresponsible flight from the issues of this world? This is a frequent criticism of eschatological faith.

Prophecy Greater than Tongues (14:1–25)

Paul gets back to the issue of the spiritual gifts in the church. Now his focus is on two of them, speaking in tongues and prophecy:

> [1]Pursue love, but strive eagerly for the spiritual gifts, above all that you may prophesy. [2]For one who speaks in a tongue does not speak to human beings but to God, for no one listens; he utters mysteries in spirit. [3]On the other hand, one who prophesies does speak to human beings, for their building up, encouragement, and solace. [4]Whoever speaks in a tongue builds himself up, but whoever prophesies builds up the church. [5]Now I should like all of you to speak in tongues, but even more to prophesy. One who prophesies is greater than one who speaks in tongues, unless he interprets, so that the church may be built up.
>
> [6]Now, brothers, if I should come to you speaking in tongues, what good will I do you if I do not speak to you by way of revelation, or knowledge, or prophecy, or instruction? [7]Likewise, if inanimate things that produce sound, such as flute or harp, do not give out the tones distinctly, how will what is being played on flute or harp be recognized? [8]And if the bugle gives an indistinct sound, who will get ready for battle? [9]Similarly, if you, because of speaking in tongues, do not utter intelligible speech, how will anyone know what is being said? For you will be talking to the air. [10]It happens that there are many different languages in the world, and none is meaningless; [11]but if I do not know the meaning of a language, I shall be a foreigner to one who speaks it, and one who speaks it a foreigner to me. [12]So with yourselves: since

you strive eagerly for spirits, seek to have an abundance of them for building up the church.

¹³Therefore, one who speaks in a tongue should pray to be able to interpret. ¹⁴(For) if I pray in a tongue, my spirit is at prayer but my mind is unproductive. ¹⁵So what is to be done? I will pray with the spirit, but I will also pray with the mind. I will sing praise with the spirit, but I will also sing praise with the mind. ¹⁶Otherwise, if you pronounce a blessing (with) the spirit, how shall one who holds the place of the uninstructed say the "Amen" to your thanksgiving, since he does not know what you are saying? ¹⁷For you may be giving thanks very well, but the other is not built up. ¹⁸I give thanks to God that I speak in tongues more than any of you, ¹⁹but in the church I would rather speak five words with my mind, so as to instruct others also, than ten thousand words in a tongue.

²⁰Brothers, stop being childish in your thinking. In respect to evil be like infants, but in your thinking be mature. ²¹It is written in the law:

"By people speaking strange tongues and by the lips of foreigners

I will speak to this people, and even so they will not listen to me, says the Lord."

²²Thus tongues are a sign not for those who believe but for unbelievers, whereas prophecy is not for unbelievers but for those who believe.

²³So if the whole church meets in one place and everyone speaks in tongues, and then uninstructed people or unbelievers should come in, will they not say that you are out of your minds? ²⁴But if everyone is prophesying, and an unbeliever or uninstructed person should come in, he will be convinced by everyone and judged by everyone, ²⁵and the secrets of his heart will be disclosed, and so he will fall down and worship God, declaring, "God is really in your midst."

Although he insists that he admires speaking in tongues (14:5), throughout this extended comparison with prophecy Paul speaks very negatively about this spiritual gift. No one likes a musical instrument that cannot play in tune (14:7–8). No one listens very long to a foreign language that one cannot understand (14:10–11). Five understandable words are better than a thousand unintelligible ones (14:19). This put-down of tongues may be Paul's reaction to a perceived exaggerated interest in this gift by the Corinthians.

On the other hand his praise of prophecy gives us insights into his sense of a healthy church. This gift illustrates communication among the members of the church. "One who prophesies does speak to human beings." Moreover, this communication is an act of "building up, encouragement and solace" (14:3). Four more times in this section Paul repeats the important purpose of building up the church (14:4, 5, 12, 17). This act is more important than speaking to God. Earlier Paul stressed the importance of "building up" in regard to the decision whether or not to eat meat offered to the idols. "Building up," placed parallel to "seeking the advantage of one's neighbor," is more important that the insight "Everything is lawful" (10:23–24). "Knowledge inflates with pride, but love builds up" (8:1). As exercised in the Pauline interpretation of this gift, prophecy is an act of love.

In this comparison, Paul tries to explain the difference between "tongues" and "prophecy" in terms of an anthropology which he may have picked up from his Stoic contacts (14:13–19). Paul contrasts "the spirit" and "the mind" of a human being (cf. 1 Thes 5:23). While the anthropological "spirit" appears to be a privileged dimension of the person for contacting God, the "mind" is the faculty for human communication. The "Amen," that others can say to your prayer is very important. It means that was also a communication with them. That "Amen" is the prayer of the Body of Christ, people praying in union with each other through their "minds," not just their "spirits."

The citation of Isaiah 28:11–12 is a bit far-fetched (14:21–22). In the Old Testament, the text refers to the Assyrian threat brought on by God to punish Israel and Judah.

The people of Judah ridiculed Isaiah as incomprehensible. So the word of God, somehow spoken through the Assyrian invaders will be incomprehensible. This is the punishment of those who "would not listen." An echo of this oracle occurs in Deuteronomy 28:49, explaining perhaps why Paul cites this text as from the Law rather than from the Prophets. From this Old Testament text, Paul concludes that "tongues" can function as an authoritative summons to non-believers (14:22).

Paul, however, then cancels the thought and reverses the relationship of "tongues" and "prophecy" respectively to "unbelievers" and "believers" (14:23–25). The exercise of "tongues" in the church would be dismissed by unbelievers as being "out of your minds," while the exercise of "prophecy" might do the unbeliever some good.

Being "out of your minds" was a real concern of Paul. He started this whole section on the spiritual gifts by contrasting the Corinthians life in the Spirit with their former life as one "constantly led and carried away to mute idols" (12:2). This is not the way the Body of Christ can suffer and rejoice together in the pain and joy of each of its members.

In his description here of prophecy (14:24–25) Paul adds something different than the "encouragement and solace" mentioned above (14:3). Here we see an accusatory and judging role of the prophet. The two roles, encouraging and accusing, are found side by side in the Old Testament prophets, depending on whether the people were discouraged by disaster or complacent in sin. Paul evidently saw a special knowledge of the heart as part of the gift of prophecy. This knowledge of the heart is normally reserved for God alone (Prv 16:2; 21:2). In any case the power of the prophet in the Christian church leads the unbeliever to confess what Deutero-Isaiah and Zechariah predicted about the Gentiles' acknowledging about Israel, "God is really in your midst"(14:25; cf. Is 45:14; Zec 8:23).

An interesting insight into the Pauline church arises from presuppositions behind Paul's description of the prophet's value for the unbeliever. Paul sees this action happening when "uninstructed people and unbelievers should come in" to the community celebration. This celebration of the gifts probably followed immediately the celebration of the Lord's Supper (cf. 11:17–34). Paul thus is drawing a boundary around the community. He speaks of insiders and outsiders, believers and unbelievers. For Paul Christian discipleship has become membership in a defined group.

That was not always the case. Jesus invited sinners to table fellowship (Mk 2:15–17). When Jesus admonished his disciples not to stop the work of the outside exorcist using Jesus' name, he gives the boundary-breaking statement, "Whoever is not against us is for us" (Mk 9:38–41). When Matthew turned that statement around, "Whoever is not with me is against me" (Mt 12:30), we see the Matthean church building walls around itself.

While Paul, however, here describes boundaries, the boundaries are porous. Outsiders can enter the community celebration. Unbelieving spouses of members are not necessarily sent away; in fact they seem to be sanctified by the believing spouse (7:12–16). The Pauline church seems to be somewhere between the all inclusive movement of Jesus and the exclusive society of Matthew.

For reflection. What would a unbeliever think if he or she witnessed our liturgical celebrations? Would they be overwhelmed with the conviction that God is in our midst? Why not? Has prophecy disappeared? Has God decided to lead his church in less dynamic ways?

Could prophecy have many forms? Are some of the prophetic functions which Paul describes still being performed by some in the church today? Imagine a prophet in your parish. He or she will function to "build up" the church. What typical actions would be accomplished by this prophet? Imagine our reaction to that prophet.

When was the last time we really said "Amen" to a prayer said in common?

Rules of Order (14:26–40)

Paul brings to a conclusion this section with a series of practical instructions regarding the community assembly of prayer:

[26]So what is to be done brothers? When you assemble, one has a psalm, another an instruction, a revelation, a tongue, or an interpretation. Everything should be done for building up. [27]If anyone speaks in a tongue, let it be two or at most three, and each in turn, and one should interpret. [28]But if there is no interpreter, the person should keep silent in the church and speak to himself and to God.

[29]Two or three prophets should speak, and the others discern. [30]But if a revelation is given to another person sitting there, the first one should be silent. [31]For you can all prophesy one by one, so that all may learn and all be encouraged. [32]Indeed, the spirits of prophets are under the prophets' control, [33]since he is not the God of disorder but of peace.

As in all the churches of the holy ones, [34]women should keep silent in the churches, for they are not allowed to speak, but should be subordinate, as even the law says. [35]But if they want to learn anything, they should ask their husbands at home. For it is improper for a woman to speak in the church.

[36]Did the word of God go forth from you? Or has it come to you alone? [37]If anyone thinks that he is a prophet or a spiritual person, he should recognize that what I am writing to you is a commandment of the Lord. [38]If anyone does not acknowledge this, he is not acknowledged. [39]So, (my) brothers, strive eagerly to prophesy, and do not forbid speaking in tongues, [40]but everything must be done properly and in order.

Paul here gives the earliest description we have of Christian liturgy. It describes a group singing, instructing each other, and praying. When Paul includes in his letter a poem, like the Ode to Love in this letter or the hymn praising Christ in Philippians 2:6–11, he may be including compositions sung at the Christian assembly. Unlike the Jerusalem church which apparently relied more on Old Testament psalms and poems (cf. Acts 2:25–28; 2:34; 4:25–26), the Gentile churches seemed ready to develop a whole new repertoire of songs and canticles.

Throughout this instruction Paul seems to insist on a wide distribution of functions. One has a psalm, another an instruction. One prays in tongues, another interprets. Prophets follow the order set by other prophets. Again Paul says nothing about who presides or about the qualifications of the presider. Paul's main concern here is wide participation of those present as well as the good order of the assembly for the building up of the church.

In the middle of verse 33, the text breaks into a new topic, shifting from the orderly functioning of prophecy to women keeping silent in the church. The statement is surprising in light of what Paul earlier said about women prophesying in the general context of church assemblies (cf. 11:5). After verse 35, the text breaks again from this topic to return to the topic of prophecy. These verses interrupt a rather smooth flowing text about prophecy. This text also refers to "the Law" as containing a specific rule for conduct which should be followed by Christians. This reference also is surprising in Paul, who frequently refers to the Law, but always as containing prophetic stories or images, never as a rule book. A few years later writing Galatians he will virtually throw out the Law as a rule book for those guided by the Spirit (Gal 5:18; cf. 3:23–29). At least two significant early manuscript copies of First Corinthians do not have these verses (11:34–35) in their present place. A number of later manuscripts follow this variance.

This evidence has led many scholars to think that these two verses were added after Paul wrote this letter to the Corinthians. This could have been done, for example, by the Corinthians who also practiced some heavy-handed editing of Paul's next letters to them. The addition could have been done by whoever wrote First Timothy, with its strong silencing of women (1 Tm 2:11–15).

During the decades at the end of the first century, the church experienced intense anti-feminism. This anti-feminism appears to have been a spinoff of a serious crisis affecting the church at that time. Internal disorders and contradictory teachers appeared in private homes of Christians, which at this time were the bases of Christian instruction and liturgy. Noble or wealthier women often took charge of the household. Anger against the disorders and contradictory teachers became directed againt the women who hosted these teachers. Those women were linked to the disorders. Both in Christian writings and in secular writings, women were saddled with the image of irresponsible religious innovators (cf. 1 Tm 5:13; 2 Tm 3:6).

Reflecting a more Roman than Greek attitude, Paul had been quite open to women exercising important speaking roles in the church, such as that of prophet (11:5). In light of the later tendency to blame women in part for the crisis of the church, a copyist of this letter probably added these two verses to bring Paul's teaching in line with the later tendency.

For reflection. We must reflect on the anti-feminist verses here. Many Christians see these verses of First Corinthians as binding *point by point* in their churches and use them as the reason for limiting the ministry of women.

The issues we need to think about sound very academic, but they have profound influence on our spirituality. One issue is that of literary genre. First Corinthians is a letter, not a systematic essay. As in our oral conversations, in letters we are often not consistent. If Paul wrote these verses, he must have forgotten what he said about women prophets. And we are then given the responsibility of understanding what the Holy Spirit is saying with such conflicting advice.

The second issue is diversity in the New Testament. If Paul did not write these verses, we can find in Paul a rather open attitude regarding women in the church, consistent with his principle, "In Christ . . . there is neither male nor female" (Gal 3:27–38). In First Timothy (and in the supposed copyist of First Corinthians) we have a very closed attitude regarding women. In part we can understand the diversity by placing the positions in diverse social contexts. In any case we see again an enormous responsibility of understanding the spiritual message of the New Testament, not just quoting texts. In fact the spiritual message of the New Testament seems to be, "Use your head!" The Holy Spirit has decided to speak through all the limits and obscurities of human discourse.

In the other matters of this section we get a glimpse of the earliest Christians assembling to celebrate and praise God. If used properly the Acts of the Apostles helps us fill out this glimpse. Meetings seemed to take place on Sundays and lasted all night (Acts 20:7–12). The meetings were experiences of the Holy Spirit. Paul's concern is not getting people interested but in keeping order.

We seem to have lost something. I see many people looking bored at our liturgies. Is the problem our hectic culture and superficial entertainment? Is the problem the way we have disregarded the gifts of the Spirit? Could we return to a view that everyone brings a gift to the assembly? Especially, could we still bring a sense of prophecy to our liturgies? When a person "owns" the liturgy, they do not feel bored. When a person understands that they are bringing a gift to the liturgy, a gift that is needed by the body of Christ, they are involved and feel it.

VIII

The Resurrection of the Dead
(15:1–58)

Without using the formula for a new question or topic as he did before ("Now in regard to . . ."), Paul starts a new subject. Whether this topic came to Paul in the form of a question or as a report of a problem, Paul's concern arises because of a denial of the general resurrection of the body, "How can some among you say there is no resurrection of the dead?" (15:12).

As he handled the issue of the Lord's Supper, Paul here appeals to a tradition about Jesus and his resurrection (15:1–11); he then shows the link between Jesus' resurrection and ours (15:12–34). Paul deals then with the question of how a corruptible body can rise (15:35–49) and concludes with an overview of the eschatological transformation in a great praise to God (15:50–58).

The Resurrection of Christ (15:1–11)

Paul begins by a reminder of the gospel tradition:

[1] Now I am reminding you, brothers, of the gospel I preached to you, which you indeed received and in which you also stand. [2] Through it you are also being saved, if you hold fast to the word I preached to you, unless you believed in vain. [3] For I handed on to you as of first importance what I also received: that Christ died for our sins in accordance with the scriptures; [4] that he was buried; that he was raised on the third day in accordance with the scriptures; [5] that he appeared to Kephas, then to the Twelve. [6] After that, he appeared to more than five hundred brothers at once, most of whom are

still living, though some have fallen asleep. [7]After that he appeared to James, then to all the apostles. [8]Last of all, as to one born abnormally, he appeared to me. [9]For I am the least of the apostles, not fit to be called an apostle, because I persecuted the church of God. [10]But by the grace of God I am what I am, and his grace to me has not been ineffective. Indeed, I have toiled harder than all of them; not I, however, but the grace of God (that is) with me. [11]Therefore, whether it be I or they, so we preach and so you believed.

The formula for an ecclesial tradition comes in verse 3, "I handed on to you . . . what I also received . . ." He identifies this tradition "handed on to you" with "the gospel I preached to you" (15:1). The intense importance of holding on to this gospel tradition appears in the way Paul connects it with salvation. For Paul salvation comes through this tradition or gospel, for "through it you are also being saved," but on the condition that "you hold fast to the word I preached to you" (15:2). Whereas Paul could be flexible on marriage and divorce (7:1–16) or food offered to the idols (10:23–33), this matter of the resurrection requires firm adherence.

In what way can a tradition, a word Paul preaches, a gospel handed on be a means of salvation? Paul consistently insists on salvation as the work of God, a work of loving grace operating through the death and resurrection of Christ, not something that is produced by human performance. He will be very clear on this in his letter to the Romans (cf. Rom 3:21–31). However, in that letter to the Romans Paul also states clearly, "The gospel . . . is a power of God for the salvation of everyone who believes" (1:16). In this light, the gospel appears less a thing that preachers preach and believers hold to, than rather the very presence of God operating through Jesus's death and resurrection to save humanity. Yet in the description of First Corinthians, the gospel is also a narration, the story of the death, resurrection and appearances of Christ (15:3–7).

For Paul, then, the gospel as preached and narrated makes the saving power of God present. In the recounting of the story of Jesus, the grace of God becomes perceptible. As power, the gospel remains the action of God. The gospel remains pure grace. Human beings enter into this grace by speaking and listening, by preaching and "holding fast to the word." Thus through this sacrament of the word, we become conscious participants of God's love, God's co-workers (3:9), stewards of the mysteries (4:1).

Paul recites the saving in 15:3–6. This text is the earliest account and witness we have to the resurrection of Jesus. Like the Lord's Supper teaching (11:23–26), this teaching was already a tradition when Paul preached to the Corinthians around A.D. 52. Actually in its present form in this letter, it appears as an amalgam of many earlier independent traditions. Thus we have the reference to Kephas with "the twelve" in one part and James with "all the apostles" in another part without any attempt to reconcile the descriptions which if isolated would be understandable but together are confusing. Paul adds to the credal statement the tidbits about who is dead and who is still alive as well as the important information about an appearance of Jesus to him. By adding his own experience of the risen Christ to the list, Paul in effect places it on the same level as Jesus' appearances to his apostles—even though Paul admits something strange about the timing.

Other elements of this credal tradition are important. The statement that "Christ died for our sins" show how the death of Christ was seen as redemptive. As we saw in Paul's description of the bread at the Lord's Supper (11:24), that little word "for" (*hyper*) carries a truckload of material for meditation. Somehow in God's plan, death deals with sin. Somehow, Christ could die "on our behalf," somehow substituting for us. The addition of the phrase, "in accordance with the scriptures" to both the death and resurrection of Jesus shows how the early church struggled to understand these events and how they found clues by correlating these events with God's plan as expressed in the Old Testament.

In the much later gospel narrative accounts of the resurrection (Mt 28; Mk 16; Lk 24; Jn 20–21), witnesses testify to the appearance of Jesus risen from the dead, not to his resurrection itself. Only in the following centuries, Christians will tell stories of how Jesus looked as he came out of the tomb. Paul's account is the briefest of all and the most sober. The resurrection itself remains a mystery unobserved. Perhaps here with the mention of the burial, the Christians could point to an empty tomb as the one historical footprint of this "eschatological event."

The gospels describe the appearances of the risen Jesus to disciples who already believe in him. In this sense the gospel tradition of the resurrection points to a "faith event." Jesus appears only to disciples, who in effect experience the risen Jesus through their faith—although often with some difficulty (Mt 28:17; Lk 24:11, 16, 38; Jn 20:24–29). Paul likewise appeals to the faith of the Corinthians as the medium through which they learn of Jesus' resurrection.

On the other hand, Paul as well as the gospel writers insist that something objective happened. When Paul describes his experience of the risen Jesus—an experience he places on the same order as that of the apostles, he depicts as it as a surprise, as something he did not prepare for, something that changed the direction of his life—a life he was rather satisfied with (Phil 3:4–6)—from being a non-believing persecutor of the church to a dynamic believer (cf. Gal 1:13–24). Here and in Galatians Paul describes the experience as either Jesus or God himself doing something, not an extension of a faith which he already had. For Paul, this was not his wishful thinking. Something happened. But Paul gives no details. The later gospel stories, like Luke's later narrations of Paul's experience (Acts 9:1–9; 22:6–16; 26:12–18), show creativity and freedom on the part of the story tellers. Paul—the only one who actually saw the risen Christ and wrote about it—is silent about the details.

In Galatians Paul describes his experience of the risen Christ like the call of Jeremiah (cf. Jer 1:5) stressing the apostolic mission that comes from it. The tradition Paul recounts in First Corinthians stresses the groups that experienced Jesus. The appearance of Jesus as Paul sees it was not a special privilege of an individual but an event within a group and an event that makes that group truly church.

Shrouded in mystery, the appearances of Jesus remain ambiguous. To the insider relying on faith, the appearances mean Jesus rose from the dead. To the outsider relying on unambiguous evidence, the apostles maybe saw a ghost or maybe nothing. Thus the appearances—like the empty tomb itself—divide people who give different interpretations to their meaning. The appearances create a bounded community. They create the faith of the church, and make sense within the faith of the church.

For reflection. We are tuning into the faith of the church before Paul. We hear of the redemptive death, the resurrection of Jesus, and of the appearances of Jesus which created a community of believers. This community in turn proclaimed this death and resurrection to other believers, just as Paul here is proclaiming it to the Corinthians. This is the gospel through which we also, almost two thousand years later, are being saved. The very meaning of our lives and our destiny lies in this proclamation.

Something happened. We hold this in faith. Jesus is alive, body and soul. As risen, he draws us to one another so that as a community we can give meaning in language to the resurrection event. We can continue to proclaim it—if only to those willing to believe. A community proclaimed this gospel and initiated us into this faith. In our lives and in our words we must continue to proclaim this gospel. The resurrection of Jesus in itself does not depend on our faith and proclamation, but it lives and transforms the minds of human beings only in that faith and proclamation.

Jesus' Resurrection and Ours (15:12–34)

The issue at Corinth is not so much the resurrection of Jesus but the resurrection of all the dead:

[12]But if Christ is preached as raised from the dead, how can some among you say there is no resurrection of the dead? [13]If there is no resurrection of the dead, then neither has Christ been raised. [14]And if Christ has not been raised, then empty (too) is our preaching; empty, too, your faith. [15]Then we are also false witnesses to God, because we testified against God that he raised Christ, whom he did not raise if in fact the dead are not raised. [16]For if the dead are not raised, neither has Christ been raised, [17]and if Christ has not been raised, your faith is vain; you are still in your sins. [18]Then those who have fallen asleep in Christ have perished. [19]If for this life only we have hoped in Christ, we are the most pitiable people of all.

[20]But now Christ has been raised from the dead, the firstfruits of those who have fallen asleep. [21]For since death came through a human being, the resurrection of the dead came also through a human being. [22]For just as in Adam all die, so too in Christ shall all be brought to life, [23]but each one in proper order: Christ the firstfruits; then, at his coming, those who belong to Christ; [24]then comes the end, when he hands over the kingdom to his God and Father, when he has destroyed every sovereignty and every authority and power. [25]For he must reign until he has put all his enemies under his feet. [26]The last enemy to be destroyed is death, [27]for "he subjected everything under his feet." But when it says that everything has been subjected, it is clear that it excludes the one who subjected everything to him. [28]When everything is subjected to him, then the Son himself will (also) be subjected to the one who subjected everything to him, so that God may be all in all.

[29]Otherwise, what will people accomplish by having themselves baptized for the dead? If the dead are not raised at all, then why are they having themselves baptized for them. [30]Moreover, why are we endangering ourselves all the time?

[31]Every day I face death; I swear it by the pride in you (brothers) that I have in Christ Jesus our Lord. [32]If at Ephesus I fought with beasts, so to speak, what benefit was it to me? If the dead are not raised:

"Let us eat and drink, for tomorrow we die."

[33]Do not be led astray:

"Bad company corrupts good morals."

[34]Become sober as you ought and stop sinning. For some have no knowledge of God; I say this to your shame.

Some Corinthians are denying the general resurrection of the dead. Paul argues against this denial by a three-part argumentation. First, he begins by pushing the denial to an absurd position, given the Corinthians' faith in the resurrection of Jesus (15:12–18). Second, he introduces a homiletic description of the end of the world, developing Isaiah 25:8 and Psalm 8:6, with allusions to other Old Testament texts (15:19–28). Third, Paul returns to the Corinthians' position to continue pushing to absurdity their denial of the general resurrection (15:29–34).

The background of the apparent reluctance of the Corinthians to believe and hope in the general resurrection of the body might well be the general Platonic view of body. For those who followed Plato in his affirmation of the spiritual and immortal soul—he called it mind (*nous*), the body was a prison. In this view, it was not really part of the human person. Once placed in the grave, it was best left there. Besides anyone who has seen a dead body—really dead, not just decorated as at a funeral—would not want it back.

Paul's answer, however, has nothing to do with philosophical anthropology. He has seen the risen Christ. He knows the Corinthians believe in Jesus' resurrection. For Paul, moreover, the bodily resurrection of Christ is not just the epilogue of salvation but an essential part of the act of God freeing us from our sins. "If Christ has not been raised, your faith is vain; you are still in your sins" (15:17). Something therefore is wrong with a denial of bodily resurrection in general.

The stress Paul makes on the link between Christ's resurrection and salvation from sin is striking. If Christ is not raised from the dead, all bets are off. Citing the tradition Paul has just affirmed the saving character of Jesus' death (15:3; cf. also 1:21–25). Redemption through the death of Jesus will be a constant theme of Paul (2 Cor 5:14; Rom 5:9; Gal 3:13; Col 1:20). Here Paul roots the power of salvation in the resurrection of Jesus (cf. also Phil 3:10). By transforming and raising Jesus from the dead, God in fact rescues all from sin. For Paul the death and resurrection belong together as the great event where God saves the world, a death to sin and a new life for God. God begins the saving event in Jesus, but Jesus is "the firstfruits" (15:23), the representative of all, the first of a series in the same order.

In the second part of this development Paul reaffirms the resurrection of Christ (15:20), introducing at least a summary of a carefully worked out homily. Paul here for the first time describes "death" as opposed to God's plan (cf. also Rom 5:12–14). In doing this he draws on a relatively recent Jewish tradition. Meditating on the story of Adam and Eve (Gn 1–3), some sages of Israel had recently seen that death itself is not willed by God but is the result of human sinfulness. Writing about one hundred years before Paul in a Greek environment, the author of the Book of Wisdom stated the position clearly: "For God formed man to be imperishable; the image of his own nature he made him. But by the envy of the devil, death entered the world, and they who are in his possession experience it" (Wis 2:23–24; cf. 1:13; for the opposite position cf. Sir 41:3–4).

If death is the consequence of sin, then Christ's resurrection is the act of God's destroying death. And, most important of all, Christ's resurrection is "the firstfruits," the first of a series, in which all who belong to Christ are included. The final resurrection of the dead then will be the moment of the Kingdom. At that moment all enemy powers, including "death," will be neutralized. This is an apocalyptic view in which Death is considered the face of sin, in which Death eventually will be destroyed in the great victory of God over evil (cf. Rv 20:14; Is 25:8).

Christ is both the firstfruits and the victorious Son. In a rare portrayal of Christ, Paul describes the Son as powerful warrior, like a military general who conquers for the king and returns all conquests to the king. Christ hands over the kingdom to "his God and Father" (15:24). Typical of Paul, however, this victory is geared for the glory of God, the Father, the initiator of the resurrection and the purpose of the resurrection.

In the third part of the development, Paul asks again the Corinthians to reflect on themselves and Paul's own life, seeing how so much of their lives and actions presuppose the resurrection of the dead (15:29–34). The Corinthians must have had a deep sense of solidarity with their dead, practicing, perhaps something like a vicarious baptism.

It is interesting that Paul's concern for the dead is couched entirely in terms of the resurrection of the body. As he wrote earlier to the Thessalonians dealing with their concern for the dead (1 Thes 4:13–18), Paul does not mention anything like a spiritual existence of the souls of the dead. He in effect states here that without the resurrection of the body any vicarious baptism would be meaningless (15:29). Writing later to the Philippians, Paul will suggest that personal communion with Christ begins immediately after death (Phil 1:22–23). In this later letter, written perhaps five to ten years after First Corinthians, Paul apparently will have adopted a more Greek anthropology in which a material part of the person can die while a more spiritual part can continue to live and experience personal consciousness. Paul will never, however, change his position about the essential importance of the future resurrection of the body (cf. Phil 3:11).

Paul points to an eschatological reference where death no long dominates us in any way, neither in spirit nor in body, where all things and all powers are again directly subject to God. At that point death will be no more. This eschatological point is not just a spiritual reality. Paul refuses to "spiritualize" salvation as a matter of getting souls to heaven. This victory involves material reality—at least the human body. Later Paul will expand his vision to include all material reality of which our bodies are only a part (cf. Rom 8:19–23). Paul thus gives us a spirituality of life and death as well as a spirituality of material reality.

For reflection. Most of us hear from our culture the message that death is a normal part of life, part of "the circle of life." The trick then is to accept death. Paul says just the opposite. Death is not the norm. Death is an enemy. We must die, but we should never accept death. As long as physical death dominates us, the kingdom of God is not fully present. As long as bodies are rotting in the grave, the kingdom of God is not fully here. Death and sin are having the last word. And that must end.

Death should be a frightening manifestation of evil. Jesus agonized before it. However, the resurrection of Jesus gives us the hope and the courage to face death. This courage is that of the Christian martyrs, who accepted death, not necessarily with stoic tranquility, but with great faith in the power of God.

Life is full of "little deaths," discouraging moments when the power of evil messes up the work of life and goodness. As Paul wrote, "Every day I face death" (15:30). The temptation is to surrender and close ourselves into a little world of immediate satisfaction, "Let us eat and drink, for tomorrow we die." Paul tells us to hold firm to the future hope of God's ultimate triumph.

The Manner of the Resurrection (15:35–49)

After a long absence the imaginary conversation partner comes back with an objection. Paul answers the objection and develops further his theology of the body:

> [35]But someone may say, "How are the dead raised? With what kind of body will they come back?"

³⁶You fool! What you sow is not brought to life unless it dies. ³⁷And what you sow is not the body that is to be but a bare kernel of wheat, perhaps, or of some other kind; ³⁸but God gives it a body as he chooses, and to each of the seeds its own body. ³⁹Not all flesh is the same, but there is one kind for human beings, another kind of flesh for animals, another kind of flesh for birds, and another for fish. ⁴⁰There are both heavenly bodies and earthly bodies, but the brightness of the heavenly is one kind and that of the earthly another. ⁴¹The brightness of the sun is one kind, the brightness of the moon another, and the brightness of the stars another. For star differs from star in brightness.

⁴²So also is the resurrection of the dead. It is sown corruptible; it is raised incorruptible. ⁴³It is sown dishonorable; it is raised glorious. It is sown weak; it is raised powerful. ⁴⁴It is sown a natural body; it is raised a spiritual body. If there is a natural body, there is also a spiritual one.

⁴⁵So, too, it is written, "The first man, Adam, became a living being," the last Adam a life-giving spirit. ⁴⁶But the spiritual was not first; rather the natural and then the spiritual. ⁴⁷The first man was from the earth, earthly; the second man, from heaven. ⁴⁸As was the earthly one, so also are the earthly, and as is the heavenly one, so also are the heavenly. ⁴⁹Just as we have borne the image of the earthly one, we shall also bear the image of the heavenly one.

This answer to the objection falls into two parts. In the first (15:36–44) Paul searches for ways to describe the difference between the mortal body and the risen body. The second part (15:45–49) is a commentary on a text from Genesis 2:7. These five verses may be another section of the scriptural homily Paul excerpted in 15:20–28 to talk about the final subjection of all enemies under Christ and God.

In the first part of the development, Paul offers examples of different kinds of bodies. The examples from agriculture or from astronomy (15:36–41) make a modern mind cringe. The best approach is to picture Paul as a person of his times, trying to find things that would make sense to people of his times and culture. The diversity in nature that Paul and his readers recognize would be all the more wondrous given the ignorance of the time. For these lines we have to try to capture the wonder without the cultural framework—as we do when we hear Jesus speaking of seeds that *die* in order to germinate.

Paul's description of the risen body and its transformation (15:42–44), however, requires a more careful look. This is not an appeal to experience as were the previous verses. This is an attempt to speak metaphorically about a key concept of his faith, the transformation of the human person which is nothing less than salvation itself. Paul gives a parallel series of contrasts which can be understood metaphorically because of some experience of the contrast:

corruptible	incorruptible
dishonorable	glorious
weak	powerful.

Because we know from experience the meaning of these terms we can see the more or less synonymous parallelism in the listing.

Paul then appends another contrast of terms for which there is no related experience, terms which appear to take their meaning from this contrast and context as well as from Paul's usage elsewhere:

natural (*psychikon*)	spiritual (*pneumatikon*).

As mentioned in our study of chapter 2, we struggle with translation here. The word *psychikos* comes from the Greek word for "soul" (*psyche*), but the word "soulish" does not mean anything and "psychic" is a worse translation. As opposed to "spiritual," we could translate *psychikos* as "natural," as long as we remember Paul is not against nature or the natural. Paul is describing something characterized by the list of synonyms in the preceding antitheses: something corruptible, dishonorable, and weak. He is describing mortality. In later writings, Paul will use "flesh" (*sarx*) to denote this dimension of life (cf. Gal 5:19–21).

The "spiritual body" then is the body with the opposite characteristics: incorruptible, glorious, and powerful. Paul is describing resurrected life. For Paul what is "spiritual" is rooted in the Spirit of God. The word "spiritual" qualifies the eschatological kingdom, although what is "spiritual" can be found proleptically now (cf. 1 Cor 2:15).

Paul here is insisting on the radical transformation of the body at the resurrection. It is different. It is not simply a return to the former life with its metabolisms. Such an insistence contrasts with some gospel portrayals of Jesus after his resurrection very much the way he was before his death (cf. Lk 24:36–43), although all the accounts describe the risen Jesus as different. Paul may be speaking from experience.

At the same time, for Paul the "spiritual body" is not simply the ghost of a dead person. *What* is sown in dishonor, rises in glory. *What* is sown in weakness, rises in power. What is sown *psychikos*, rises *pneumatikos*. What is sown is the body. Therefore, the dimension of continuity between this world and the eschatological world is the body.

In the second part of the development, Paul uses some homiletic material to provide another contrast. Here Paul cites Genesis 2:7 and applies a non-biblical Jewish story to elaborate the meaning. That story arose from the observation that God created the human being twice in the creation account, at Genesis 1:26–27 and at Genesis 2:7. In the non-biblical Jewish story, the first account describes a heavenly man created as an archetype for humanity. The second account describes the earthly counterpart. Paul in his homily reverses the order, identifying the "heavenly man" with Jesus, who obviously came after Adam. This story has little to do with the resurrection, but it does provide another contrast between heavenly and earthly things, and so Paul "cuts and pastes" it into his letter.

For reflection. In the risen body, Paul wants us to see the power and glory of the Kingdom. This is what Jesus' death and resurrection is all about. It happened to Jesus first. It will happen to all of us. In the risen body we see God's victory over sin. This risen body is nothing less than "a new creation," as the apocalyptic writers would write. Only God can bring this about. The foundation is here laid for Paul's later teaching about salvation through grace not works (Rom 3:21–31).

We see in this description also the stress on transformation rather than destruction, on continuity between our mortal body and the risen body. Our body is capable of this transformation. That makes our body important. As Paul wrote earlier in this letter, even now the body is already a Temple of the Holy Spirit *within* us (6:19).

Thus the transformation is not just future. If we are "in Christ" already, we are beginning the transformation. Little by little Paul will be clearer about the nature of the present transformation as a renewal of the mind or the inner life (Rom 12:2). Writing Romans he will speak of the process already begun because we have already died with Christ (Rom 6:3–5). Eventually—if Paul in fact is the author of Colossians—he will write that we are already risen from the dead (Col 2:12).

Living now on earth the life of the future resurrection thus becomes the great challenge of Christian life. The Spirit dwelling in our bodies puts us into this paradoxical situation, where our decisions now should reflect the power and glory and honor of the eschatological Spirit. The Spirit dwelling in our church bodies should make those communities beachheads of the eschatological kingdom.

The Great Transformation (15:50–58)

With lyrical tones Paul reviews the scene of this eschatological transformation climaxing with the praises of God:

⁵⁰This I declare, brothers: flesh and blood cannot inherit the kingdom of God, nor does corruption inherit incorruption. ⁵¹Behold, I tell you a mystery. We shall not all fall asleep, but we will all be changed, ⁵²in an instant, in the blink of an eye, at the last trumpet. For the trumpet will sound, the dead will be raised incorruptible, and we shall be changed. ⁵³For that which is corruptible must clothe itself with incorruptibility, and that which is mortal must clothe itself with immortality. ⁵⁴And when this which is corruptible clothes itself with incorruptibility and this which is mortal clothes itself with immortality, then the word that is written shall come about:

Death is swallowed up in victory.
⁵⁵Where, O death, is your victory? Where, O death, is
  your sting?
⁵⁶The sting of death is sin, and the power of sin is the law. ⁵⁷But thanks be to God who gives us the victory through our Lord Jesus Christ.

⁵⁸Therefore, my beloved brothers, be firm, steadfast, always fully devoted to the work of the Lord, knowing that in the Lord your labor is not in vain.

As a summary description of the end of the world, this text connects in theme back to 15:20–28 (cf. also 1 Thes 4:13–18). As a theological development citing scripture, the text continues the Adam commentary just preceding and continues the homiletic style, especially with its climax in the scriptural "double-whammy," the practice of concluding a homily with a pair of texts (cf. also 1 Cor 3:19–20).

The opening statement about "flesh and blood" not inheriting the kingdom makes Paul at first sound like that of a pessimistic rigorist. The expression "flesh and blood" was an expression for "human beings" as contrasted with God (cf. Mt 16:17). Down deep, however, this statement might be one of the most hope-filled statements of Paul.

Earlier in this letter Paul wrote repeatedly, "The unjust will not inherit the kingdom of God" (6:9). Later in Galatians after listing the works of the flesh he will write, "Those who do such things will not inherit the kingdom of God" (Gal 5:21). These statements are really full of fire and brimstone, coming out of the typical apocalyptic portrayal of the final separation of the bad from the good and the ultimate consignment of the bad to hell—often to the delight of the good guys (Rv 19:1–3; 20:15; Mt 25:41).

Paul's exclusion of all "flesh and blood" from the inheritance, however, breaks the bounds of apocalyptic form. "Who then can be saved?" the apostles asked, when Jesus came up with a similar ironic statement about the impossibility of salvation (Mt 19:24 and parallels). Jesus answered by pointing out the omnipotence of God. Paul answers by pointing out the universal transformation of humanity, "We will all be changed. . . . That which is corruptible must clothe itself with incorruptibility, and that which is mortal must clothe itself with immortality" (15:51, 53). This is the work of God. This transformation does not occur during one's lifetime. This is a change that is nothing less than the resurrection of the dead. Paul's exclusion of "flesh and blood" is not a restriction of who will be saved but rather of the need for God to transform us before we can inherit the kingdom. Perhaps we should read the other "will not inherit" statements in the same way.

The universal scope of this salvation appears in Paul's comment, "We will all be changed" (15:51), This is the change "in the blink of an eye" from corruptibility to incorruptibility. Earlier in the chapter he stressed the universal character of this salvation, "For just as in Adam all die, so too in Christ shall all be brought to life" (15:22). It is hard to read any restriction into the "all in Christ" statement given its parallel with the "all in Adam" statement, which clearly embraces all humanity. Paul presents no scenario of a division of the good from the bad (cf. Mt 25:31–46). Paul described much the same thing earlier to the Thessalonians, when he was speaking of being "caught up together . . . in the clouds to meet the Lord in the air," where "Thus we shall always be with the Lord"(1 Thes 4:17).

Thus arises the victory song. Paul cites a special Greek form of Isaiah 25:8 along with the text of Hosea 13:14 (15:54–55). Again Paul associates death with sin. The association of "the Law" with sin, however, is a surprise (15:56). While this will be the unifying theme of Romans and Galatians, Paul has said nothing really negative about the Law up in First Corinthians or any other letter he has written earlier. It is very hard to figure out what Paul means here by identifying the Law with "the power (*dynamis*) of sin." One sense that Paul himself uses of the Greek word, *dynamis*, is "meaning" or "significance" as in the *dynamis* of a language (1 Cor 14:11), in which case Paul is saying that sin expresses itself through the Law. Still the lack of explanation here turns this line into a type of "soap box opera" ending, which keeps us moving into the next installment.

Paul attributes this victory over sin to God, who operates through Jesus (15:57). It is God, the Father, who must be praised by this future but present victory. God is the savior.

These thoughts about God's power to overcome evil, God's power and plan to transform all of us, should not inculcate in us a sense of complacency. Paul ends with an exhortation to hard work (15:58). He holds up the possibility of laboring "in vain" (*kenos*) here, just as he held up the possibility of believing "in vain" at the beginning of this whole treatment on the resurrection. Paul is balancing his theology—which suggests universal salvation—with his pastoral care—which worries about complacency. It is a difficult balancing job.

For reflection. The thought of "universal salvation," is the idea that we will all make it to heaven, those who were good with those who were bad through the power of God, perhaps transforming us at the last second. Do you think Paul really held this thought?

Pastors rarely preach the theme of universal salvation not because they explicitly deny it but because it could lead some to a sense of complacency and presumption. It could be "pastorally imprudent." Could the thought of universal salvation lead some people to this complacency and presumption? Could it be for some a strength and encouragement to live a good life?

Sometimes people will object to the idea of universal salvation because it seems to offend their sense of fairness. Picture a really "despicable" person to heaven. Something seems wrong in that picture. But what is wrong? Remember the anger of the "good son" in the parable of the prodigal son (Lk 15:11–32). The father had to explain his love for all his children. The love of God for his children might be so intense, we can never understand it. What is wrong with the picture of "universal salvation" is our inability to include the incomprehensible love of God into that picture.

We have seen crowds clapping and cheering at the execution of "despicable" persons. Once in a while the news gives us a picture of the anguished parent of the "despicable" person being punished by death. Which picture do you think better represents God's love?

IX
Letter Conclusion
(16:1–21)

The final part of First Corinthians consists of a series of short instructions and exhortations, mixed with Paul's travel plans. All of this is typical of Paul's ending a letter. Sometimes the most interesting part of these short instructions are the presuppositions, stuff we can read between the lines. Other elements are interesting because they help us reconstruct the history of Paul and his letter writing.

The Collection (16:1–4)

Paul reminds the Corinthians about a monetary collection to benefit the members of the Jerusalem church:

> [1]Now in regard to the collection for the holy ones, you also should do as I ordered the churches of Galatia. [2]On the first day of the week each of you should set aside and save whatever one can afford, so that collections will not be going on when I come. [3]And when I arrive, I shall send those whom you have approved with letters of recommendation to take your gracious gift to Jerusalem. [4]If it seems fitting that I should go also, they will go with me.

The progressive development of this collection, mentioned here, in Second Corinthians 8–9, and in Romans 15:25–33, helps us place these three letters in chronological order. Paul here is organizing the collection. In Second Corinthians he says he is coming to pick it up. In Romans he says he has it. Acts knows about such a collection but seems to have placed it much

145

too early in Paul's career (cf. Acts 11:27–30; 12:25). The importance of this collection ties into Paul's desire to acknowledge the priority of the church of Jerusalem, the mother church, the "holy ones," the Jewish Christians who guarantee the permanence of God's promises to Israel (cf. Rom 11:1–10). Paul's promise to Peter, James, and John "to be mindful of the poor" (Gal 2:10) is almost certainly an acknowledgment of the priority of the church of Jerusalem.

The "installment method" of collecting the money for Jerusalem hints at the "middle class" character of the Corinthian church. The very wealthy could move money as they wished. The very poor had no money to collect.

The reference to "the first day of the week" might be the earliest indication of the Christian use of Sunday to celebrate the liturgy. A liturgy corresponding to the descriptions of community prayer in this letter would be a good time to get the money together. Later, Acts 1:7 will explicitly connect the "breaking of bread" with the first day of the week. The Book of Revelation describes "the Lord's Day" as the time of the visions (Rv 1:10), probably also a new Christian name for the "the first day of the week."

Paul's Travel Plans (16:5–12)

Next Paul gives his plans for visiting the Corinthians:

> [5]I shall come to you after I pass through Macedonia (for I am going to pass through Macedonia), [6]and perhaps I shall stay or even spend the winter with you, so that you may send me on my way wherever I may go. [7]For I do not wish to see you now just in passing, but I hope to spend some time with you, if the Lord permits. [8]I shall stay in Ephesus until Pentecost, [9]because a door has opened for me wide and productive for work, but there are many opponents.
>
> [10]If Timothy comes, see that he is without fear in your company, for he is doing the work of the Lord just as I am.

[11]Therefore, no one should disdain him. Rather, send him on his way in peace that he may come to me, for I am expecting him with the brothers. [12]Now in regard to our brother Apollos, I urged him strongly to go to you with the brothers, but it was not at all his will that he go now. He will go when he has an opportunity.

Travel plans are frequent in Paul's letters. They serve to remind us that these writings are letters, inferior substitutes for oral communication. The geographical details of this section correspond well to what Acts 19 says of Paul: he is in Ephesus, he has already visited Corinth once, and he is on his way to visit the church there a second time. This correlation with Acts 19 suggests Paul is writing this letter around A.D. 55 on his third missionary journey.

We can only wonder why Paul thought it was necessary to tell the Corinthians not "to disdain" Timothy. He never says that about Titus. Was Timothy a bit of a "wimp"? Paul had already mentioned the sending of Timothy at 4:17.

Apollos, mentioned in connection with the factions in the Corinthian church (1:12; 3:4.22), seems to be on good terms with Paul. But Apollos is a person who makes his own decisions. There is no military chain of command yet in the leadership of the church.

Final Exhortations and Greetings (16:13–24)

Before Paul ends the letter, he pours out a barrage of advice and greetings:

[13]Be on your guard, stand firm in the faith, be courageous, be strong. [14]Your every act should be done with love.

[15]I urge you, brothers—you know that the household of Stephanas is the fruitfruits of Achaia and that they have devoted themselves to the service of the holy ones—[16]be subordinate to such people and to everyone who works and toils with them. [17]I rejoice in the arrival of Stephanas,

Fortunatus, and Achaicus, because they made up for your absence, [18]for they refreshed my spirit as well as yours. So give recognition to such people.

[19]The churches of Asia send you greetings. Aquila and Prisca together with the church at their house send you many greetings in the Lord. [20]All the brothers greet you. Greet one another with a holy kiss.

[21]I, Paul, write you this greeting in my own hand. [22]If anyone does not love the Lord, let him be accursed. *Marana tha*. [23]The grace of the Lord Jesus be with you. [24]My love to all of you in Christ Jesus.

These last words of Paul in the letter sound like someone reluctant to hang up the phone. Maybe Paul just had a few more blank inches on his expensive papyrus. It is clear, however, that Paul likes the Corinthians and likes to talk to them.

The initial splatter of exhortations stresses strength (16:13). Paul wants them to take on their role of "the mature" and the strength that goes with it. Acting with love says the same thing.

We get a hint of local church structure with the mention of "the household of Stephanas" (16:15). The advice to "be subordinate" (16:16) is clearly an allusion to leadership and authority in the local church. The basis for this leadership, however, is seniority and dedication of this household. There is no mention here of "laying on of hands," as will occur later for the designation of leadership roles. Stephanas is obviously at the center of this leadership, but his whole household is mentioned.

Aquila and Prisca with their "house church" send their greetings (16:19). They were from Corinth where they had a house big enough to host Paul and his workers (Acts 18:1–3). As mentioned in Acts, they were originally from Rome, whence they were expelled by the edict of Claudius. They soon will be back in Rome with another "house church" when Paul next makes mention of them (Rom 16:3–5).

Reference to the "holy kiss" suggests a liturgical gesture perhaps like "the kiss of peace." If this letter is meant for the whole church of Corinth (1:2), a prayer gathering would be a convenient place for such a letter to be read out loud.

The triple prayer wish at the end begins with the Aramaic expression *Maran atha*. This is a prayer, "come!" (*atha*), "our Lord" (*Maran*). Paul, a Greek-speaking Jew, writing to a Greek-speaking church is using an Aramaic expression. This preservation of the Aramaic expression indicates the "traditional" nature of this prayer, rooted in the Jerusalem Christian community. The return of Jesus was on the mind of the Christians from the beginning. It is at the heart of Paul's gospel for the Corinthians.

For reflection. This chapter in the letter is about people. We see here Paul surrounded by people, concerned about people, giving news about people. Look at all the names we have from this chapter. These are our "fathers" and "mothers" in the church. The decisions they made in faith during their lifetimes made the church as we know it possible. Some of them appear rich, like Aquila and Prisca. Some look like propertyless itinerants, like Timothy, Apollos, and of course Paul himself. Stephanas may have been powerful head of a household; Achaicus, a slave. (It is a slave name.)

Paul says, "Be strong! Act with love!" Apparently they did because we have a church in which to celebrate, proclaim, and be part of the death and resurrection of Jesus. "My love to all of you."

Further Readings

Commentaries

Barrett, C. K. *A Commentary on the First Epistle to the Corinthians* (New York: Harper and Row, 1968).

Collins, Raymond F. *First Corinthians*. (Collegeville, MN: Liturgical Press, 1999).

Conzelman, Hans. *1 Corinthians. A Commentary of the First Epistle to the Corinthians,* trans. J. W. Leitch (Philadelphia: Fortress, 1975).

Fee, Gordon D. *The First Epistle to the Corinthians* (Grand Rapids, MI: W. B. Eerdmans, 1987).

Grosheide, Frederik W. *Commentary on the First Epistle to the Corinthians* (Grand Rapids, MI: W. B. Eerdmans, 1979).

Harrisville, Roy A. *1 Corinthians* (Minneapolis, MN: Augsburg Publishing, 1987).

Kilgallen, John J. *First Corinthians. An Introduction and Study Guide* (New York: Paulist Press, 1987).

Murphy-O'Connor, Jerome. *1 Corinthians* (Wilmington, DE: Michael Glazier, 1979).

Soards, Marion. *1 Corinthians* (Peabody, MA: Hendrickson, 1999).

Studies

Clark Wire, Antoinette. *The Corinthian Women Prophets. A Reconstruction through Paul's Rhetoric* (Minneapolis, MN: Fortress Press, 1990).

Furnish, Victor Paul. *The Theology of the First Letter to the Corinthians* (New York: Cambridge University, 1999).

Hurd, John C. *The Origin of I Corinthians* (Macon, GA: Mercer University, 1983).

Martin, Dale. *The Corinthian Body* (New Haven: Yale University, 1995).

Mitchell, Margaret M. *Paul and the Rhetoric of Reconciliation. An Exegetical Investigation of the Language and Composition of 1 Corinthians* (Louisville, KY: Westminster/John Knox, 1993).

In the Same Series from New City Press

Mark
From Death to Life
Dennis Sweetland
ISBN 1-56548-117-8, paper, 5 3/8 x 8 1/2, 216 pp.

Matthew
God With Us
Ronald D. Witherup
ISBN 1-56548-123-2, paper, 5 3/8 x 8 1/2, 216 pp.

Romans
The Good News According to Paul
Daniel Harrington
ISBN 1-56548-096-1, paper, 5 3/8 x 8 1/2, 152 pp.

Paul's Prison Letters
Scriptural Commentaries on Paul's Letters to Philemon,
the Philippians, and the Colossians
Daniel Harrington
ISBN 1-56548-088-0, paper, 5 3/8 x 8 1/2, 136 pp.

Revelation
The Book of the Risen Christ
Daniel Harrington
ISBN 1-56548-121-6, paper, 5 3/8 x 8 1/2, 168 pp.

Daniel
A Book for Troubling Times
Alexander A. Di Lella
ISBN 1-56548-087-2, paper, 5 3/8 x 8 1/2, 232 pp.

Song of Songs
The Love Poetry of Scripture
Dianne Bergant
ISBN 1-56548-100-3, paper, 5 3/8 x 8 1/2, 168 pp.

To Order Phone 1-800-462-5980
www.newcitypress.com